SUDOKU

MEDIUM TO HARD

ZIGZAG PUZZLE VOL1

NAME :________________________

START DATE :________________________

END DATE :________________________

How to solve Sudoku puzzle?

1.A total of nine squares must contain nine numbers from 1 to 9 without overlap.

	7							4
	2	4	6		9	7		
				5				
6	9				8			1
5				2				7
		3	4		1	2		
1	3			6	2			8
2					5			
	5	8		3			9	2

2.A total of nine horizontal lines must also contain nine numbers from 1 to 9.

	7							4
	2	4	6		9	7		
				5				
6	9				8			1
5				2				7
		3	4		1	2		
1	3			6	2			8
2					5			
	5	8		3			9	2

3. A total of nine vertical lines must also contain nine numbers from 1 to 9.

	7							4
	2	4	6		9	7		
				5				
6	9				8			1
5				2				7
		3	4		1	2		
1	3			6	2			8
2					5			
	5	8		3			9	2

Medium Puzzle 1

DATE: TIME: ~

	7							4
	2	4	6		9	7		
				5				
6	9				8			1
5				2				7
		3	4		1	2		
1	3			6	2			8
2					5			
	5	8		3			9	2

Medium Puzzle 2

DATE: TIME: ~

2	4	9			7		3	
	7	1					2	
			2			5		
7		3	9					
	2	6	4	7				5
		4		8		2		
			1	6				
8				4	3	1		9
	1	5		2			6	

Medium Puzzle 3

DATE: TIME: ~

		6					4	
4					6	5		
3						9		6
		9	3	8				
	8		7			3		
	3			5	1			
	2	5	4	9	7	8	3	
8		7	1	3			5	
1				6		4	7	

Medium Puzzle 4

DATE: TIME: ~

		7			2			1
						8		
2				9				3
					8		9	5
9			4		1	3		
				5	7	4	1	2
3	2		8	7				
	4			2	6	5	8	
6		8		1	4	2		9

Medium Puzzle 5

DATE: TIME: ~

8							1	6
9	2		3			5		7
				9	4	3		
1							3	
	7	8	1	5		2		
				8			6	
4	3	2						9
		1		2			5	
	9	7				6	8	2

Medium Puzzle 6

DATE: TIME: ~

5				3			1	
	8					7		
		2	8	4		3	6	
			3					8
2	9		4	7				
		8	5		6			
	4		6		3	9		
8		3		5	9			6
	7				4	5		2

Medium Puzzle 7

DATE: TIME: ~

		5	7		4		3	
7	3					2		
6	1		3	9		5		4
2	8	6			1		4	
		1	5					8
					7	1	2	
					3			
8			1				5	3
1			2				6	

Medium Puzzle 8

DATE: TIME: ~

3			1				2	
		7	2	6		4		
	2	4		8	9		1	
		3					9	5
8				4	2	1		6
5				9			7	
9								2
	3				5	9	4	
7		5					6	

Medium Puzzle 9

DATE: TIME: ~

							1	
			4	8	1			
7		1			2	3	4	8
3					7			1
			5		4			2
		8	2	1		5		3
9	1	5	6	4				
	4			2		9		
6		3					5	

Medium Puzzle 10

DATE: TIME: ~

		1	9		7		4	8
	6		5	3				9
2						6	3	
		6		5	9			
					3		6	
4		3		8			9	
			8				2	
3		7	1				5	6
	2			9		4	1	

Medium Puzzle 11

2 DATE: TIME: ~

2	8		6		9		5	7
	6						8	9
		7				6		1
9		8	1			4		
	5				7			3
6		2	3					
		3				8	2	
5			8	3				
				5		1		

Medium Puzzle 12

DATE: TIME: ~

5	4							1
	2		4		1		7	
		1	8	7			2	
					7		1	3
				1	3		6	2
1			2	5				
	7	3			8	1		
	1	8						9
		5	1			8		

Medium Puzzle 13

DATE: TIME: ~

1		4			5			2
					2		9	
			9		1	6	5	
9			1		8		2	3
4		8						
				6			7	
		2		9	6	3	4	
		9	8	5				1
5	3	6				7		

Medium Puzzle 14

DATE: TIME: ~

5	9	1		2	6			8
				1			2	3
6	2				4			
				4	2			
4							7	
8	7		6			5		
	4	7	5					1
1				3	7			9
2			4			3	6	

Medium Puzzle 15

DATE: TIME: ~

			3	1	2		7	
	7					2		
4	2			9			8	6
							9	1
	3					7		8
			8	5	6	3		
		1	2			9		
7			9	6	8	5	1	
3			7	4	1			

Medium Puzzle 16

DATE: TIME: ~

		7	6		3	8		2
				7		4		1
	4			2	9			3
		8	9			3		
	3				5		4	
		5	2					
9	5						1	8
6	2	3			1		5	4
			4	5		6		

Medium Puzzle 17

DATE: TIME: ~

			6			4		9
4	8						1	
	5		7	3				
7			4		3	9		1
	3	9			6			
	1							
1		7		2		8	9	4
2		5			9			3
	9	3				5		6

Medium Puzzle 18

DATE: TIME: ~

5	6			3				
			6			2	8	
9			2		5			1
3	2	9			1			
6	4		5	7	3	9		
					9	6		
7		6			2	4	3	
		1					7	
	3				6			

Medium Puzzle 19

DATE: TIME: ~

5							6	
8	2		1	3				
	6			9		8	1	2
		4			9	6		
3				8		9		
	5		3		1	7	4	
	4				3			
		1	2				7	
2				5			3	

Medium Puzzle 20

DATE: TIME: ~

		7			5	9		
5	6				7	2	4	
	4	8	3	2			6	
	1	5	8					7
8					2	6		9
	9				4	1		
4	8	6	9					
7						3		
		3	4		1	8		

Medium Puzzle 21

DATE: TIME: ~

4	7		9		2		8	
2		3	7				4	9
				8		5		7
			8					
5	6			3				
	1	4					6	
3	4			9	1	7		
9					8			2
	2			5	4			

Medium Puzzle 22

DATE: TIME: ~

		5	3				7	1
3					6	5		
	4	9			7		3	6
				2		9		5
		2				3	4	
		3		9			1	2
8				4				
	6				2	7	5	4
	3		9					8

Medium Puzzle 23

DATE: TIME: ~

	4	2			5	3		6
		5			3	1		
1		9	6		4	5	2	
	9		2	4				
3		7	8	5		9		
							6	
8			7					
	5	6	4			2		7
		4		1				

Medium Puzzle 24

DATE: TIME: ~

	1	4			9	2		
			5	3			1	
	7					5		
		3	4	7		6		1
				2	6	3		
8		9			1			7
			1					
9			7		2		5	
1		5		9		7	4	6

Medium Puzzle 25

DATE: TIME: ~

		1		9		2	3	4
2	7							
	8	4	3				5	6
	6	2	5		7	3		
7		5					1	
			2			6		
		8		7	6			
					5	9	4	7
1	9							8

Medium Puzzle 26

DATE: TIME: ~

		7	6			8		
				2	4	1	6	3
	4			1			5	
6	1			7		9		
5			9	3	2			
		2				3		
	7	9					3	
			5		6		2	8
2							1	9

Medium Puzzle 27

DATE: TIME: ~

					8	5		
7	5			9	3			6
		3	7		4	9		
3			5				6	
	2			8			3	
4			1					8
	3	2	8			4	1	7
	6			7	1	3	9	
	4							

Medium Puzzle 28

DATE: TIME: ~

	5	1	3					7
9			1			5		4
7						9		
4				1	6	2	9	
		2			5			
6			7	2				8
5			9	3		4	1	
	1			6		7		
			2			3	5	

Medium Puzzle 29

DATE: TIME: ~

			6	7		5	4	3
			9				8	
					5			1
		5		4	9		2	
9	6				7	8		
3						4		
1			2		8		7	4
4		3	7	6	1	2		
	7				4	1		

Medium Puzzle 30

DATE: TIME: ~

5		9		8	6			7
3		7			2			
			3	7	9			4
			1		4		3	
			9	6		7		8
		1	7	2				
			6	9	7	4		
		4	2	3				
9					1	5		3

Medium Puzzle 31

DATE: TIME: ~

3				5	2			4
7	9			4			5	
4		5			9			
	7		3			6		1
6			1	2			4	
			4				8	7
	3		5				2	
9				6			1	5
8			9				3	6

Medium Puzzle 32

DATE: TIME: ~

			1		6		5	
6	7	3		2				9
			4	7				2
3		5	6				2	
7					1	5	9	
							4	8
		2		1	8		3	5
5	6				9	2	8	1

Medium Puzzle 33

DATE: TIME: ~

7	9				2	3		5
			5		3		1	
	3	8		6				
	1	2			4			
	5		7	9		2		4
							8	
2	6	7		5				
	8	5		1				3
1			9			8		7

Medium Puzzle 34

DATE: TIME: ~

	9		8	3		1		2
						7		
	4	6						3
6					8			
				5		9		
9	1	3				4		8
			2	8	1	5		
7	2				5		1	
1	3	5	4	7	6			

Medium Puzzle 35

DATE: TIME: ~

		4					7	3
5			2	6	9	1		4
	8	9				5		
2	9	3					5	
	1					2	3	
7		5				8		1
	7		5		3	6		
			7					5
	5			8	4		9	2

Medium Puzzle 36

DATE: TIME: ~

			1	7			2	9
	2			4			7	
		5		2	3			4
8	4			6		2		
3	6	9	5	8				
	5				9		8	
	1	6			4		5	
		8	7		6	1		
4	9	2						

Medium Puzzle 37

DATE: TIME: ~

			9			1		2
	6		3			9		
9	8	5	1			4		7
			7	2			1	
	7	6				5		3
5	9		6			7		
	2			7				6
4					6	8		5
			4		9			

Medium Puzzle 38

DATE: TIME: ~

8			6	4			9	
	5		1				8	7
4	2	1				5		
		8		9				
2				3				
			2	1			5	3
		2	3			1	4	
1		4		6		9	7	
9	8	7						

Medium Puzzle 39

DATE: TIME: ~

	2		3	9		6		1
		8		5				9
4	6	9		8				3
					5			
	4	2			9	7	5	
7	5							2
	1			7				
						8	6	7
		3	5	6	2		1	

Medium Puzzle 40

DATE: TIME: ~

2		8	6	1				
	5	6			7			1
			8	9		7	5	
	8	9	2	6			4	5
3				5	1		6	
		1	3		6		2	7
	6	2				5	3	
						6		4

Medium Puzzle 41

DATE: TIME: ~

			5				9	3
	3		6			5		
		2	3	8	4			
				2				8
3	5						6	7
		6	7					
					9		3	
8		4	1	3	5			9
	7		4				2	

Medium Puzzle 42

DATE: TIME: ~

6						8		2
9		5						
8	2			7			1	
3				9			2	4
	4			6		1		3
		1	4	3		6		
			7				4	8
	6		5	8	3	2		
	3		9				7	6

Medium Puzzle 43

DATE: TIME: ~

8		1						
6	2							7
	3	4			8			2
	1			2	6			9
9				7			8	
		7	8				4	
	8		2	9			3	
4		2				7	5	
3		6			1	9		

Medium Puzzle 44

DATE: TIME: ~

1	7				2	5		
3			9				4	
		9		7		3	6	
5		2		6	1			7
4					3			9
8	6		7				2	
	3							5
9	5		1					
		4		8			1	

Medium Puzzle 45

DATE: TIME: ~

							2	1
	8		1			9		6
3	5		9	6			4	
			7	8				3
1				3	9			
		3				2	7	
	9	8	5		3			
7					6	3		5
	3	6			7	8		

Medium Puzzle 46

DATE: TIME: ~

4						8		
	2		9			6		
5	6			1	2			9
2				3				
			7	2	6	4		
8		6			5	2	9	
				7			6	
		4			8		2	1
	8	9			1	3	4	

Medium Puzzle 47

DATE: TIME: ~

		7		1		2	6	4
		2		4	9			
6	1					8		
9			7		1			6
	2				8	5		3
			5		6		9	2
7			1		2			8
					5		4	
3	8					6		

Medium Puzzle 48

DATE: TIME: ~

	8					4		5
		1			7	3	6	
2	6	3					8	7
	4	9		1			7	
	1		9		3	2	4	
				6				
8			4				3	
1		2				5		
	7			9	2		1	8

Medium Puzzle 49

DATE: TIME: ~

	8	9	7	2	4			
				8		9	6	
5		4			9			7
						6		
		1	4	3			9	
7					1	4		
		3	6	4		8	7	
			8	1		5		
2				9			3	6

Medium Puzzle 50

DATE: TIME: ~

			9	1	7			
	3	8		4			1	
2		1					5	9
	8			3	4	2		
	2	4		6				
		7				3		8
	5		4		2		3	
1	4	3	6			5		
			1			6		

Medium Puzzle 51

DATE: TIME: ~

	8						7	4
5				4		1		
6		9		2	1	3		5
7		5		6		9		
	9				7			
3	1	6	5	9				
		8	1		4		3	
4	6				2			
2		7					5	

Medium Puzzle 52

DATE: TIME: ~

		3	6			1		9
		1		2	9			
		2	4	8				
	4							
6				1	3			7
			8		4	2		
9	7					5	4	
2		5	7	4		8		1
	1		2			3	7	

Medium Puzzle 53

DATE: TIME: ~

	4			9	3	5		
			8			2		4
		8	4	6			7	9
4		6	5			3		
2	8				4			5
	1		9	2				
		5	1				6	
		2	7			9	5	3
	3		6				2	

Medium Puzzle 54

DATE: TIME: ~

4	9							
	3		4	5				6
6	5			7			9	1
		7	5	4			1	
		9		6			3	
3		5		8				2
	1		7				4	8
				1		6		
	2	3					7	5

Medium Puzzle 55

DATE: TIME: ~

			8	6		1		4
9				2		8	6	
				1	4		7	
		9			3		2	8
	8	4						6
6	2					9	3	
					9	6		2
2	9		5					1
		8			1	3		

Medium Puzzle 56

DATE: TIME: ~

					3		1	5
		3			5			4
		4	7			2	9	
6	2						3	
	1	9	6	3		5		
	5	7		4				6
9		1	3					8
7				8				
		2	9		4	3	7	

Medium Puzzle 57

DATE: TIME: ~

		3	6			1		9
		1		2	9			
		2	4	8				
	4							
6				1	3			7
			8		4	2		
9	7					5	4	
2		5	7	4		8		1
	1		2			3	7	

Medium Puzzle 58

DATE: TIME: ~

		3	9	2		5	4	
9			1			7		
		7						
	2		5	4		6	3	
	3		7			2	5	9
6	8			9				
5	6	1			4		9	
						8		5
			6				7	

Medium Puzzle 59

DATE: TIME: ~

		5		1		2	7	
7	6	3			5			
				7				5
5	1			9		4		3
	9	4				5		7
					8		9	
		7	2	8				
6		2						8
9	8		5	4	7			

Medium Puzzle 60

DATE: TIME: ~

	1		9		6			
	8			2				
				5			6	3
				6	2	7	3	
7			3					1
5						6	4	
2			6		9	3	1	
	3	7		8		4		6
		1		3		9		2

Medium Puzzle 61

DATE: TIME: ~

	3			2		4		
1	6	5		7				
				8	1			7
5	1				6		7	
				1				2
		6	8			1		3
					4		2	1
	4	1	2	9	7	5		
6						3		9

Medium Puzzle 62

DATE: TIME: ~

3							6	9
8				5		1		2
				8			5	
5	4		6					
		8		2	1			5
9			8		5	7		
1		6	4		9	5		
4	5	3		6		9		
	9	2				6		

Medium Puzzle 63

DATE: TIME: ~

6	8				1	2		
	2						4	5
			5			3	6	
4		3	8	1	6			
				7			8	
			2			7	1	6
1		6		8				4
			3			6	9	1
5	9			6				

Medium Puzzle 64

DATE: TIME: ~

6	2	9		5				7
				7	9	2		4
	5			1	3		8	
	4	3	1			8		
		1	9					
					7			3
	3	4					2	
			8			3	6	
8	9							1

Medium Puzzle 65

DATE: TIME: ~

		7			2			8
			3	9		1		
					8	3	7	
	4				5			
	2	9	6	1			4	
1	7			8	9	2		
7	9			5				
	5	6			1	8	2	
3	1	8					5	

Medium Puzzle 66

DATE: TIME: ~

		7		6		8	3	5
6					7			1
5	4			3		2	7	
2							8	7
			9	8	1			3
8	9	6	2		3		5	
4		9	7		6	3	1	
3			4					

Medium Puzzle 67

DATE: TIME: ~

7		4				6		
		3	9	1		7		
2					4		5	8
	5	7		6	2			
1			5	8		2	3	
		8						9
8			1		3		7	6
	3		4					
		5				9	1	

Medium Puzzle 68

DATE: TIME: ~

	6		4	5		2		3
		1		7		5		9
						7	4	
				4		6	5	
	7							
	5	2	7					1
			1		2	4		
8				3		9	6	
6			8				7	5

Medium Puzzle 69

DATE: TIME: ~

		6						
			8		3	4	6	7
4			7	6	9			
					6	3	7	4
3	5	7		4				
	4	1					2	
								8
			3		5	2		
	3	8		7	1		9	

Medium Puzzle 70

DATE: TIME: ~

	5	8				6		
4	1			8				
3		2	5		9			
		1	8	6				7
				7	1	4	2	
			9					
9	2	7	4		8			3
6		3		1	7			5
	8			9			7	

Medium Puzzle 71

DATE: TIME: ~

	5		9		7	1		
8	9	1						
			4			5	6	
		7		2				
1			8	7	3	2		6
	2		1		4	8	7	
	7	4						1
9					8			2
	6				2	9		4

Medium Puzzle 72

DATE: TIME: ~

					5		1	
1	8	6	4					
					1			7
8		9			2	4		
3				5			8	
	5					3	9	
		7	8			2		
6	9		5	7			3	1
			9	2	3		6	

Medium Puzzle 73

DATE: TIME: ~

3	4	9				6		2
			2	6	8			4
				4				
1			7	5	4	8		
6	7	8					5	
5		4		3	6			7
	1				9	7		6
4		6			5			
							4	

Medium Puzzle 74

DATE: TIME: ~

9	4	1	8	2			7	5
			1				9	4
7		8						
2	1							7
		7		3	8			
					4	5		
			4	6			2	9
	7				2	1		6
		4				7		

Medium Puzzle 75

DATE: TIME: ~

4		6	3					
			9				3	
5					2			
				9	3	2		1
			4					7
	8	7		6				
3	2	8		1		6		9
	5	4			9	3		8
1				3	7		5	2

Medium Puzzle 76

DATE: TIME: ~

8								9
		5					6	7
	6						3	1
7		4	3				8	
			4		7		2	5
9	1	2			8		7	
1	4			8	6			
2		6	9		1			8
	9			3	2			

Medium Puzzle 77

DATE: TIME: ~

	5		3	6			2	4
		2	5		9		8	
	8			2				
7	6	5		4				3
			9					
3		4		7			6	
5					4	8		
		9	2		1	3	7	
	2			8			5	

Medium Puzzle 78

DATE: TIME: ~

				3	8		2	
	7	6				3		8
	5					9		
	1	2			9	4		5
4		9	1					
	2	8				6	3	4
	6			4	2		7	
	4			8	1	5		2

Medium Puzzle 79

DATE: TIME: ~

		8		5	4		9	
			9	8				2
	9		3			7		
		9		1				3
	7	2			5	4		
	3	1				6		
2								7
9	1	4				8		
7	5	3	8	9		1		4

Medium Puzzle 80

DATE: TIME: ~

	9				5	2	6	8
	6	8		1		7		
7			9			5	4	
		5		3		8	9	
					4	6		
1			8	9	7			2
	8	7			6			4
6	1		2		9			
					3			

Medium Puzzle 81

DATE: TIME: ~

	7		2		1	6		
	3		9	8				7
						1	8	
	6				7		4	3
5	8			9		2		
		9	6	3				1
				2				
				6	5	7	9	8
8			4	1				2

Medium Puzzle 82

DATE: TIME: ~

	3				2	5	6	4
4	1					9		
			9	3				
5			6	4			9	
9		7	3			4	5	
			5	7		3	8	
2		6	1		3			
							7	2
		4			7	1		

Medium Puzzle 83

DATE: TIME: ~

	8				7	2		5
6	3	5					7	
				3		1		
4	2		1			5		3
				7	4	8	1	
8			5		3	7		
9	5			8				1
			3	4			5	7
					2			4

Medium Puzzle 84

DATE: TIME: ~

		1			2	7	9	8
8								
5		7					6	3
		3	8		4	5		
	5		6			9		
4	7	6						1
7				4		6		
9	3	5					1	2
	8		9		1		7	

Medium Puzzle 85

DATE: TIME: ~

9	8			1			2	5
	3							
7					6		9	1
	7				3		5	
		2	8				4	
4	1	9	5					
			2		4	6		8
1				9				4
		4	7		1	2	3	

Medium Puzzle 86

DATE: TIME: ~

6			8		1		5	
				4		6		
	2	5		3			7	4
		6		9				
2				7	8		9	3
		7	5	1		2	6	
		2				5		
		9		6	7			
	4	8			3			

Medium Puzzle 87

DATE: TIME: ~

					3			
	2					5	7	4
						1		6
5		1			2	3	6	
				9			8	
6	8		4		5			1
7					1	8		
1				5		9	4	
	9	5		7		6		2

Medium Puzzle 88

DATE: TIME: ~

			8	2	4			6
				1				
		5					3	2
5	3				1	2	7	8
1				8			4	
				3	7		1	
	5			4				
	6	8	2					
9		2	1	5	3		6	4

Medium Puzzle 89

DATE: TIME: ~

	9	7			2	4		8
8		3	1	7	9	6		2
		1					3	
5								
		6	2				8	
9			7	5	8	3		1
3	1		6	2		9		
	5							4

Medium Puzzle 90

DATE: TIME: ~

8		5			7	4		
1				9				8
			4					2
2				7			6	
4		9	6					
					8	2	1	3
5	7	1	2	6			3	
		3		1		7		
9						6		1

Medium Puzzle 91

DATE: TIME: ~

3							5	
						8		
5		4		6	8	1		
	6			1	9			8
			4	7				2
1	7		8		6			
9		5			7	3	6	
	4		6		1	9	8	
			9	8			2	7

Medium Puzzle 92

DATE: TIME: ~

	7				9			
3	8			7				2
2		9		6				4
8		3	2			9	6	1
	2	1	8				5	
5							3	
	1	2			5			
	3	5	4	8				
9					2			5

Medium Puzzle 93

DATE: TIME: ~

	9							
6		4	2				5	3
2				4		7		
		6		7	4	2		5
		3	6					7
		2		1	8	9		
		1		6	3			9
	6		5			4		1
	8			9			2	

Medium Puzzle 94

DATE: TIME: ~

	6	4	1	7		3		
2		9		6		8		7
1			9	2				
						6		
			2	4				1
	1	5				9		4
	3					1	8	
			8		1	4		5
5	8				4	2	7	

Medium Puzzle 95

DATE: TIME: ~

		4			3			6
		3	7					2
	6		4	2	8		3	1
	4	5						
		1				6		3
3	2		1			9		
		8	9	5			6	
6							4	5
5	3	7			1			

Medium Puzzle 96

DATE: TIME: ~

2			4				3	
	3		1			5		
	4	7		9	5	2	6	
6								
		2				9	1	6
		1			7		8	
3			7	1				9
			2		4	6		
			8	3		4		1

Medium Puzzle 97

DATE: TIME: ~

					9			8
	9		1	3	5		6	
		7					3	
5	8				1		2	7
					4			5
2		1	3		8		4	
8	4	9						
	2	6		9		5		4
7		5		4				3

Medium Puzzle 98

DATE: TIME: ~

	5			6	9	3		8
		9		3		7	4	5
8			5		7	6		2
				1			2	6
6			4	8			5	
5	9							
				2			6	
1				5			3	
	8	2	1					

Medium Puzzle 99

DATE: TIME: ~

	7					9	8	
	8		1				6	2
			5	2				
		5					9	7
9	3							
1	6				5	2		4
	4				1		2	6
	1		2	9			5	
		8	3	4	6			

Medium Puzzle 100

DATE: TIME: ~

					1	7		2
	1		4		6			
	7	4	8	5		9		
			1				2	
	8	1			7	4		
	9	7	2	8	3		1	
	5	3						8
		9		3		1	5	
		6				2	3	

Medium Puzzle 101

DATE: TIME: ~

7		6	9		2			4
			3	7	5	6	2	
			1		6			8
6	7			3		4	1	
				6		5		7
1				2			8	
9		8			4			
		5	2					
4	2		8					

Medium Puzzle 102

DATE: TIME: ~

2		3		7	6		5	1
				9		6	2	
	1		4					
					8			5
5		1			7			
	7	6		2		3		
	8		1	6			7	3
		7						6
			7		3	2		4

Medium Puzzle 103

DATE: TIME: ~

1			3		9			
5			6			9		7
		9			5		1	
6							5	9
			5	6	4	8		
		5		2				
	3		1	4		2		
9	1			5			7	
4		2	8	9		6		

Medium Puzzle 104

DATE: TIME: ~

		3	6	4		7		
	1			7		5		3
7	9	4				6		
6			4		2			1
			3	5		4		
	3	2					7	
	4			6			3	
	7				1			
2	6				4			8

Medium Puzzle 105

DATE: TIME: ~

	1		2		6		9	
4			9	3		1	8	
9		3	1	4				
1		4	7				6	
	5	2		1				7
6	3					8		
3			8			6	7	
		1		6		2		
		8	3	7			5	

Medium Puzzle 106

DATE: TIME: ~

	8			9			3	7
	9	6			1		2	
		7		8		1	6	
					8	6		
	4	2		1	9			5
8	5		2	6		3		
4	7			5			8	
2			1		6			
								3

Medium Puzzle 107

DATE: TIME: ~

8	5	1	7					6
	3	2			6	1		
				1	3		8	9
6				7				
	8		2				3	4
			4	3	5		7	
3			1					2
		6		8				
2	7					8		3

Medium Puzzle 108

DATE: TIME: ~

			2	4		8	6	
4		7		3	1			
					8		7	1
		6		7		9	2	
5		4	9	1				
3	9				5		4	
	6			5	9			
			4			7		
	4					5	8	6

Medium Puzzle 109

DATE: TIME: ~

	3						8	7
	1				8	9	3	
					9	5		
3								2
	8	4	5			6		9
		1	7		2		4	
	4	9	3	6			2	
7			1				9	3
1			9		4		6	

Medium Puzzle 110

DATE: TIME: ~

	8						5	7
2					8			
	9	7		1		6		
	1		7		2		9	8
8	4						2	
9			4		5		1	
	3			2	4			
7		8					4	3
4	5	1	9					

Medium Puzzle 111

DATE: TIME: ~

5	6		8	3		1		
8				7	1		5	3
1				4	5		6	
2				1		3		5
			5			6		
4					3		9	1
	3	2		5			8	
					7			
		8		2		7		4

Medium Puzzle 112

DATE: TIME: ~

		7	5	6				
			2					
	6			4		5	2	
		3	9	1			4	7
1		8		7			5	
7		4						2
						4	7	
8	7				9	2		3
3	4				7			5

Medium Puzzle 113

DATE: TIME: ~

2			6	7			4	
5		7					6	3
					5	7		
		8		9	6	3	7	
	4			5		2		9
9				1		5		6
7		5	3			4		1
			1			9		
4					7			

Medium Puzzle 114

DATE: TIME: ~

7			4	6		3		
9			5				7	
6	8		7	3		4		5
					3	1		
8	4	1			7		5	3
			1	5	4	8		
		3		8	5	2		
		6		4				
	2							4

Medium Puzzle 115

DATE: TIME: ~

8		4		5			9	2
			7	9				
9		3	6				5	
2				7	6	8		
		6			9	5	7	
1			5			9		
	5	1					4	
		8		2	7		1	
	2				5	7		8

Medium Puzzle 116

DATE: TIME: ~

3		4	2	1		6		7
	2		4		6		1	
		6			5		9	4
			8	6		3	4	
			9	4	7			
				2		8		
1		2		3			6	
	7	9			2			
		8						1

Medium Puzzle 117

DATE: TIME: ~

2			1	6	4	7		
			5			1		8
	1						6	
		6	7	3				
3	5	7	2				9	6
		1		4		8		
	7	8				6	4	
		2		5				3
4				2			7	

Medium Puzzle 118

DATE: TIME: ~

4		5	8					
				4	1	5	3	
		7					4	
7				3				
8			4		6	7	2	
	4				9			
3	8		7	9				4
9	5		3					8
2				8		1		3

Medium Puzzle 119

DATE: TIME: ~

9	4						6	
5	8		3		1	4		2
	3	6						8
	2	3	4					
			1	8				9
		8	2					5
	1			3		7	5	
4								1
		5			7	9	2	4

Medium Puzzle 120

DATE: TIME: ~

	1			8				3
3					2	9		
	9	2	3			4		
				3				7
		6			7		5	4
8					4			
4		7	9		1	5	8	
			6		3			1
	5			7		2	3	

Medium Puzzle 121

DATE: TIME: ~

			8		4			
	7	1	3		6	9		
	4						5	8
			1		5	8	2	
	6		7			5	1	
2						4	3	7
		6	5			7		
	2				3	1	6	
		3			9			

Medium Puzzle 122

DATE: TIME: ~

	2	7		5			8	
	3		4		2			7
	9					2		
2				1	7			9
	1		9		4	7	5	
		9	5	8				
			7			8	1	3
		4				9	2	6
	6	8		9				

Medium Puzzle 123

DATE: TIME: ~

	5							4
		7			4	8		2
			6	9			1	7
3		5	4	8			7	6
7	9			5		3		
1	8	4	7	6				
		2		3	5	7		
		9						
6					2			

Medium Puzzle 124

DATE: TIME: ~

				5	2	3		
	9				7	1	4	
				8				2
5	3			9			2	
	8	9	2					
		2			6			8
8	5			7				
		6	8	4	1		7	
7				2	9			4

Medium Puzzle 125

DATE: TIME: ~

6				3			4	
7	8						1	
	2	4		1		6		7
					1		8	
	5	8	4		2	1		
	7	2	9					
							7	
5								3
8	3	6	5	4		9	2	

Medium Puzzle 126

DATE: TIME: ~

			7		1			8
3	6		5	9	8	4		
	2		6			5		9
		3	4		2		6	
			9	7			8	
2	5	7	1			3		
	9				7			2
		2					4	3
1								6

Medium Puzzle 127

DATE: TIME: ~

2	8	1	7					3
		4			2	5		
	5			4	3	2		
	1				8			9
	2		1			4	5	
		3	4				8	
				8		3		5
	4				9		2	1
9		5			1			

Medium Puzzle 128

DATE: TIME: ~

	7	4	5			3		2
5		6	1		3		7	
1				4		8	5	
								9
		9	2		5	7		1
					4		6	5
		3		9			4	
7			3				9	
		5		7		1		

Medium Puzzle 129

DATE: TIME: ~

		9				3		8
6		3		5		7	4	
	2	1		8				5
3	6		9			8	2	
						9		
1		8	3	7	2		5	
	5	6						
		2		6	7		8	
					4			9

Medium Puzzle 130

DATE: TIME: ~

	3		5		4	1	8	
	1						5	
5		8				3		6
2			3		7		1	
	5		4	8			6	3
				1				
9	2	5		4				
3		7	1		8			2
8			9			5	7	

Medium Puzzle 131

DATE: TIME: ~

6	2				8			7
		8	6		7			1
				4				9
8		1	7					
			8	9	5		6	
9		2				5	7	
				7	3			
					4	7	1	
1		6	5			2	4	3

Medium Puzzle 132

DATE: TIME: ~

	5							
2		6	9			5		1
4	8		5					
8	1		4		9			6
6		5			1	3	8	4
		4	6	8		2		
				6			3	2
9				5	4			
	2	1					6	

Medium Puzzle 133

DATE: TIME: ~

	2	5		6	3			
7		8						6
9					1	7		5
				7	6	5	8	9
		3					2	4
6	5			4	8		7	
	9		1	3				7
3	1		6			4		2
						1	6	

Medium Puzzle 134

DATE: TIME: ~

1		6		8	2		3	
5			1		9	8		
	8			6	7	4		
	6					2	5	
					6			8
9				1	5		7	4
		8		5			6	
			2		3			
2				9		7		3

Medium Puzzle 135

DATE: TIME: ~

				1	6	4		3
7							1	
	8	1				7	6	
	7	5		6	2	3		
		6	9			8	7	2
					8		5	4
	9			4				
	1			5	3		4	8
		8			7		3	

Medium Puzzle 136

DATE: TIME: ~

9		3			4			
	1		5					
7			2	6		9		5
1					3		4	
	2		9	7	6	8		
							6	
	7	1		5				4
	3	9			7		8	
6		2	1	9	8	3		

Medium Puzzle 137

DATE: TIME: ~

	1		2		3	4		
	4		8			6		9
				6				
8					2	9	3	5
7		5		4	8			
			6	3				
	2	1			6	5	7	4
	5	6		2	9	3		
		7			1			

Medium Puzzle 138

DATE: TIME: ~

	2	8	9				7	1
		6		3				
		4			2			3
2	9		4			5		
	8		7		5		2	
	6	5		2				
5				9	7		4	6
		7		1	6			2
	1		2				8	

Medium Puzzle 139

DATE: TIME: ~

	3					5	7	
		8	9					
2				1				
		3			5		8	7
5	8					6		2
4	9	6	7					
				7	4			1
				2	3	7		9
7		2			9	4		8

Medium Puzzle 140

DATE: TIME: ~

							1	
	2	9		7				6
7	3		6		8	4		
	4		9	6			8	
		6			2	3		
	1	7	5				9	
3	7	2	1					
		8	4					7
9			7	8	3			1

Medium Puzzle 141

DATE: TIME: ~

					9		6	
7	8	6	3	1	4			
				5			3	1
	5			3		9	8	7
2	7				6			4
9								2
8	9		5	6	1			
	6		8					5
	1	7						

Medium Puzzle 142

DATE: TIME: ~

								2
	5				8	7	4	
6	9		2			5		
4			7				5	8
			8		4	6		3
3				5				9
		9	4	8		1		7
	6	1					3	
2		7	9					5

Medium Puzzle 143

DATE: TIME: ~

4		6	5	7				
2		3		9		5	7	
5				8				
		9		3				1
		4	9					7
	7					6	9	5
9	2	1			4	3	5	
			8					
6				1	5		2	

Medium Puzzle 144

DATE: TIME: ~

		8						
	3			1	5		8	
2					4		7	
						9	6	
	9		6	2		4	3	8
		7					1	
3		2			6	7	4	9
6			2		3		5	1
	1				9	3	2	

Medium Puzzle 145

DATE: TIME: ~

					5	9		6
7		4			8			3
	8	5		2				
		8	1			5	7	
	6					1		9
1				3	7	8		
9		1		6		3		8
	2	3		4				5
					3	7	2	

Medium Puzzle 146

DATE: TIME: ~

		2				3	7	
1		3			9	4		8
6	7	8						5
		1			5			
	6		4	8				3
3			9		7	6		
2	9		5			8		7
5				9		1		
				4			5	2

Medium Puzzle 147

DATE: TIME: ~

	5				2			6
6		7		5			2	9
2	1	8	6	4				
	7				4			5
	6		1		5	9		8
	9			3	7	4		
1				7				
	2	6		9				
	3	9				2	5	

Medium Puzzle 148

DATE: TIME: ~

			6			3	9	
3			9	2				4
9		5	4	1		6		
		4					8	2
			7	5		9		
1							7	
		6		4		2	3	
				8				9
8	1		5				4	6

Medium Puzzle 149

DATE: TIME: ~

8							9	
					9		8	4
		2			7	1		
3						8		5
		4	9					3
6	2			3	1			7
				9		3		
	7	1	2			4	5	
	8		1	5				9

Medium Puzzle 150

DATE: TIME: ~

		4						
1			5		4		3	2
				6		5		8
5	6		3		8		2	
	4	8		1	9			6
	1		6		5	7		
			2					
	2	5	1				7	
	7						6	5

Medium Puzzle 151

DATE: TIME: ~

6	3					5		
8	1	4	5			3		
5		7		3		4		2
		5	3		8		9	4
4				6				8
9				2			7	3
			8					
2				9		8		
	4							6

Medium Puzzle 152

DATE: TIME: ~

		4				8		2
			2		7		1	6
	7	6		1				
	1	2	8					3
		5	6	2			4	
9						5	2	7
3					1			
			4	6	3	7		
	5		7	9		3		

Medium Puzzle 153

DATE: TIME: ~

	8		3			2		
	4	7						3
		1			7			
	9				6	1	5	2
5				2		8		
	2	4		5	8			
7		2			9		4	8
		5	6		1			9
				4				1

Medium Puzzle 154

DATE: TIME: ~

9	2		1		8		7	
	6	5		7				
		1		2	9		8	
4		8				1		
6		7		1	2			9
2		3		9				
	8				1	6		
		9		3				5
	4	6	9					3

Medium Puzzle 155

DATE: TIME: ~

		3	9					
		9	5	1		8		
	5							9
8				2		9		
				5	6	7	4	
					3	6		
3	1	7		4				8
	6	2			1			7
9	4			6			2	

Medium Puzzle 156

DATE: TIME: ~

3				4	9	5		
	4	5					3	
		8	5					6
1				8			7	4
			1	2				
9						8		
6		4			5	3		
	7		4	6	3			
5		2		9			4	7

Medium Puzzle 157

DATE: TIME: ~

4			9					
	9		8				5	2
7	6							
9		4				3		5
		1		3		6		
			4	1		2		8
8	1						2	
				2			8	
3	5	2			6			1

Medium Puzzle 158

DATE: TIME: ~

			8		9	1	3	5
2		5		7				8
8	1		4					
3				5				
4				6		2	7	
9			2			8		3
	6		3		7		9	
	9					7	8	
	8					3		4

Medium Puzzle 159

DATE: TIME: ~

1		3		2	4			
				1			7	4
					9		1	3
3	8		6		7	1		
4					1	5		
	1		3				4	6
9	6	1						7
	5	4		8				
	3						6	9

Medium Puzzle 160

DATE: TIME: ~

			7		2			
4	6	2		5	8			1
		7			4	3		
1					6		4	
		4						2
2				3			9	6
8		3	2			6	5	
9			1					7
			5	8		2		

Medium Puzzle 161

DATE: TIME: ~

			1		3			6
	7				9		5	1
					7		4	
5	2	8		4				3
3	1		2		5	4		
	4		9	3				5
		7					3	9
	6			9			1	
9			8				6	4

Medium Puzzle 162

DATE: TIME: ~

8		7					1	
			7			4		6
			4	8	5	7	2	3
				5		8		9
	9	3					7	4
7	8	6					3	
		8			3			
3		1		4	2	6	9	
	7			9				

Medium Puzzle 163

DATE: TIME: ~

	3			5			4	
5	8	1			9	2		3
6			2	1			8	9
	4		3		5	8		6
	6							
		8	9		2	3		
3	1				7			
8			4		6			5
		6					9	

Medium Puzzle 164

DATE: TIME: ~

					2	5	3	6
		9	7	5				
	2	3			4	7		
	9					8	5	
2				6	9	4		
	7				8	2		
				4			7	5
		7	3	8		9		
	1	6	2	7				

Medium Puzzle 165

DATE: TIME: ~

5	4	2				1		6
				3			4	
3	7			4			8	
6		8		1	3		2	7
		4	7		6	9		3
2	8				9	7	1	
	9				8			2
			4		5			

Medium Puzzle 166

DATE: TIME: ~

			1			5		
	7			6	3			4
5		3		2	4		7	1
	9	6			1		2	
	2						1	
4		1		5			3	
2			8			3		7
			7	4				
8			3	1			4	6

Medium Puzzle 167

DATE: TIME: ~

1			9	3				2
					5		8	
9		5	6	8			3	
			5			8		
	9	3		4		2		
7	1			6			9	5
	3					9	5	
					4			6
		1		7	9	3		

Medium Puzzle 168

DATE: TIME: ~

			3	6		8	4	5
	4	1			7	3		
	3							
3			9		2	1		7
		6					5	2
	7					4	8	3
1	6		2	7	4			
8				5				9
			1			6		

Medium Puzzle 169

DATE: TIME: ~

	5	4	9				6	1
7								
1				6		8		9
	2				9	5	3	
			6	1		9		
		9		5				
9	6	7	2				4	
	1		5		4	6		2
	4					3	8	

Medium Puzzle 170

DATE: TIME: ~

5					7			2
		1		8				
		7				5		9
	3		5					
	1	5		4				8
9		2				6		7
			9		8	2	6	
8		4		1				
			4		3	8	1	5

Medium Puzzle 171

DATE: TIME: ~

		5		7				
3	9		8	4			7	6
7	6	4			9	8		
		7		6		5		
1			5					
		6	1					8
	2		9				1	
5		8			1			9
		1	3		6			4

Medium Puzzle 172

DATE: TIME: ~

		7	4	3			2	8
3	8			5		6		
2	5							7
	3			6		7		1
5				9	8	3		2
7	6				3			
				4	2			
4	2							5
		9	8		5		4	

Medium Puzzle 173

DATE: TIME: ~

	4		1		7	2		3
		7		9	3			
8	3	1				6		
		4	7			1	9	
	7	8		4	1			
	5			6				
	1		4				8	
	8	6	9			5		
4	9		3				1	

Medium Puzzle 174

DATE: TIME: ~

							3	9
			1	7	9		6	
2								8
	6	1			8			
8				5	1			
5			4	9		1		7
	8	2			4		7	
3	9			1	7	5		6
	1		9		2			

Medium Puzzle 175

DATE: TIME: ~

1		7	6	4		2		
		9	5					
2		5				7	4	
		4	8					1
		6	3	1	2			
	2	1	4				6	8
							5	
6			9	5	1			2
4		2	7			8		

Medium Puzzle 176

DATE: TIME: ~

	2	1						9
					3		1	
			1			3		
7	5			9			8	
4			5	2				1
2		3			4		9	6
8		4	2		9		5	
		9		4		6		8
	7		6			9	4	

Medium Puzzle 177

DATE: TIME: ~

	4						7	
		2			4			3
9	8	3	6	2	7			
							3	
	1		7					
	2		5	4	3			9
		5	8	9		4	6	7
7		8	4	1				
	9					8		1

Medium Puzzle 178

DATE: TIME: ~

		4		3	6	8		5
	9					7	6	
5	7		8		1	4	3	
	4		2		5			
	8			6	3			9
7		3	1					
	3	5					4	
				5	2			3
	6		3	4	8			

Medium Puzzle 179

DATE: TIME: ~

			3	4		7		
8	7	9	1			6		4
	6		9	7			2	
3						2		
6		7	8	1				3
1		4	2			9		
2				8			7	
9	8			5		1		
				9				

Medium Puzzle 180

DATE: TIME: ~

				7			4	
	8	9	6					
2		1			5			
	2			1				7
5		6		2		9	3	
		4		5	7		2	8
				4	2			
6		2						
	3			6		1	7	2

Medium Puzzle 181

DATE: TIME: ~

5		3		7	9		8	
	8			2		3	9	
9	7				6	5	1	
					7	1		4
7	1						6	8
	4					2		
		7	6		3			
				8	1	6	4	5
8			5			7		

Medium Puzzle 182

DATE: TIME: ~

2	6	9	3	5			4	8
	1	7			4			
							9	7
5		6						
	4				2	9	6	
		1	8	6			7	
6			1		3			
7				9		3		
1	3		2		8		5	

Medium Puzzle 183

DATE: TIME: ~

	3			8				9
	7	8		2	1		6	4
	6			7	3	8		
4		7			2			
3		5			9		2	1
6	2					7	9	
	1		2		6		4	
2					8			
		3	4					

Medium Puzzle 184

DATE: TIME: ~

9	1		8					
	3	6			1	8	4	7
		5				1		
7	4				9	2		
		3	2	1				
			7	6				5
	7		9					
				3	2		5	1
3					6	9	8	4

Medium Puzzle 185

DATE: TIME: ~

3					4	9		5
6		4		8	4	1		8
9		8		7		4	3	5
7	9		1	6	2	1		2
6	4	2	1			9	9	6
		6	7	4	9	5	7	8
5	2		4	9		6		
1		3		6	8	7		
2		9	5		8	8	9	1

Medium Puzzle 186

DATE: TIME: ~

3						9		
6					4			8
9		8						5
7	9				2	1		
		2	1				9	6
		6		4	9	5	7	
5			4	9				
1		3		6				
2		9	5		8			1

Medium Puzzle 187

DATE: TIME: ~

3	4		6	7				
		7						1
		6	5		4			
	3		8	5	9	1		
7	6		3			8	9	
		9					3	4
	7		4			9		
1					8		7	6
	2						1	8

Medium Puzzle 188

DATE: TIME: ~

5	1		4	7		8		6
8			5				7	
4			8	2	6			3
	8		2	3	4		1	
		1	6	8				
6					7			
1	6	2				7		
	4					1		
7						5		1

Medium Puzzle 189

DATE: TIME: ~

	5			1			3	
9		3	6		2		5	4
	1	2		3		7		8
3			7				8	
			1				4	7
		6	5	4		3	1	
	9	5			6			3
				9		8	7	
	3					6		

Medium Puzzle 190

DATE: TIME: ~

7	6	8				5	4	
4	5				7		9	
1	2				5			8
			9	5			3	
			7		8	9	5	1
9			4	3		7		
6						2		
		1			4		6	5
5	7			6				9

Medium Puzzle 191

DATE: TIME: ~

	8				1	7		
6	7				9			
		3					1	2
			8	9	2	1		
4				6				
		7	4	5		8	2	
8			3		5		9	
7			9	4				
	1	9				3		8

Medium Puzzle 192

DATE: TIME: ~

	1			8			5	3
	3	2					7	
5		8	7					
1	6				2	7		
8		7		6		3	1	
			8				9	4
2		3			9	8		
			4					7
4		1	3	7			6	9

Medium Puzzle 193

DATE: TIME: ~

			4	9	2		1	
			5		7	8		
		7		6		2		4
	7					9	8	
	3					7	2	
6			8		3	1		
7		2			5		9	
9							6	
5			6		9			1

Medium Puzzle 194

DATE: TIME: ~

	4						5	8
3		1	5			6		4
			6	4	9	7		3
5			8	9			3	
			7	3	2			
					6	2	8	
						5		
9	8	7	2		5	3		
		4			7		6	

Medium Puzzle 195

DATE: TIME: ~

		4						
	9		2			7	1	
7				4	5	2		
	8		6			9	3	
		7					2	
		9	3		8			
3	6		5					1
2	7			1			9	3
			7			5	8	2

Medium Puzzle 196

DATE: TIME: ~

	6		1				7	
7	5	2		3	8		6	1
			7			3	2	
5	8				1	6	4	
			4			5		
	2			8	9		3	
4					5		8	6
			6				1	
		6			3	7		

Medium Puzzle 197

DATE: TIME: ~

1	3						5	
8			7				9	
9					1			8
			2		6			
	2						6	5
6				4	5		7	3
		5		1	2	9		
3					7	6	2	
	7	6		3	9		8	1

Medium Puzzle 198

DATE: TIME: ~

		9		6			4	
1			4	9	5			
	7		3				1	
				4		6	3	
		1		7		8	5	2
		2	9	5			7	
				2			8	1
			7		6			5
2		5						3

Medium Puzzle 199

DATE: TIME: ~

	3		2		7			
1		7		5			4	
	5	6	3				7	
				7		2	3	9
	1		4				5	
2		5					1	4
3	4		7		6	8		
		2		8	3		6	7

Medium Puzzle 200

DATE: TIME: ~

5			1	3	4			7
		9				3	1	
3	1		2	8		6		
9			8		7		3	2
4		2		9				
	7							9
	9	4					5	1
			9		8		6	
		1				8		

Medium Puzzle 201

DATE: TIME: ~

6	8	7		9				
		2	6		7	4	8	
		9		1	2			5
	6	1		5	4			
7	9				8		1	
1				8	3			
	4	5	7		9	8		
	7		2		1			

Medium Puzzle 202

DATE: TIME: ~

9			6		7			2
				8				4
		8		2		9	6	3
			7	5	2			9
1		5			9	6	8	
3			1					
		7						8
4	6				5	2		
8			3			5	9	

Medium Puzzle 203

DATE: TIME: ~

6	3					7		5
			5					6
	8	2	9				1	
		8	3	7		1		2
9					2			3
		3	4		5	9		
3			1			6	8	
1			2					
8	5	4			6			

Medium Puzzle 204

DATE: TIME: ~

			9		1	7	5	3
	1		3	5				9
				6			8	
		6			8	3		2
	5	3		2		8	9	
1	2		4					
	7	9			2	5		
	8			7				
5				3		4		

Medium Puzzle 205

DATE: TIME: ~

		6					4	
4					6	5		
3						9		6
		9	3	8				
	8		7			3		
	3			5	1			
	2	5	4	9	7	8	3	
8		7	1	3			5	
1				6		4	7	

Medium Puzzle 206

DATE: TIME: ~

3				5	2			4
7	9			4			5	
4		5			9			
	7		3			6		1
6			1	2			4	
			4				8	7
	3		5				2	
9				6			1	5
8			9				3	6

Medium Puzzle 207

DATE: TIME: ~

			3					
4	3						6	
2	6	7		4			1	3
	1	8	6	5	9			
3	2	5						6
					7	8		
			1			6		5
1				9		7		
	7	3	8	6		1	2	

Medium Puzzle 208

DATE: TIME: ~

1								2
	8	2		7	9			
3		9	5	6				
						4		
			6	9				5
8		1		4	5			
	2				7	6	8	1
7				2		9		3
	4			3	1	5		

Medium Puzzle 209

DATE: TIME: ~

	5		6		8			
9					2	5		
1	3	8	7			2	4	6
3	4	7						
2			5				1	
		6	8			9		
8	7	3	2		1			
		5						3
4					5		6	

Medium Puzzle 210

DATE: TIME: ~

			3	9			5	
								6
			2				8	
6	4			7	8		1	
				2			7	
1		8				4	9	2
9		6			4	2		1
		3	8		2			
		7				8		

Medium Puzzle 211

DATE: TIME: ~

8			7				9	
	1	6	3				8	5
5								
1		5	6			9		
		9	1	2	5	6	7	
		7		9	8		5	1
					7	8		
			9		1		2	4
	2			6				

Medium Puzzle 212

DATE: TIME: ~

	1				5	4	6	
		9			6	7	2	1
			7		1		9	3
					7		8	
7	9			6		3		
5		6	9	4				
1			6			2		4
9				7		8		
	3			2			5	

Medium Puzzle 213

DATE: TIME: ~

		4				8		2
			2		7		1	6
	7	6		1				
	1	2	8					3
		5	6	2			4	
9						5	2	7
3					1			
			4	6	3	7		
	5		7	9		3		

Medium Puzzle 214

DATE: TIME: ~

	5				7		6	4
			8			3	1	2
1	2			4	3	5		
				8	2			6
3					6			
	6			3				9
	3			2				8
5	9		7		1	2		
	7						9	

Medium Puzzle 215

DATE: TIME: ~

9		7		1				3
			2	8	7	9		4
4	8			9	5			7
			5	7	8		1	2
	3		1					
5							8	
			4		6			
2	7			3		5		9
8								

Medium Puzzle 216

DATE: TIME: ~

9					6			7
				9		4	6	
		6		1			9	2
6	2		5	8	4	1		
		4		2	3			
1		8					5	
		1				7		8
4			6		8			1
5	8		3					6

Medium Puzzle 217

DATE: TIME: ~

3		7						
			3		1			9
	9	6		5	4	3		
								6
				8	5			
5	2		9	6			1	
8	7	1		9			6	3
			5	3	8		9	7
	3		7			2	4	

Medium Puzzle 218

DATE: TIME: ~

	1			9	5	3		
	3						8	
6					3	2		9
2	6	4	3			5		
7		8			2	9		
				5	6	4		2
4				3		7		
1		3	9					
5	8	9		2				4

Medium Puzzle 219

DATE: TIME: ~

								7
	9		5	7	6			8
		3		1	9			
		5			1			2
4		1	3	9			7	
8							1	3
	1	8		2	4	7	3	
	6			3		8		
			1			2		6

Medium Puzzle 220

DATE: TIME: ~

	9	7			2	4		8
8		3	1	7	9	6		2
		1					3	
5								
		6	2				8	
9			7	5	8	3		1
3	1		6	2		9		
	5							4

Medium Puzzle 221

DATE: TIME: ~

		4	9				1	2
					2			
	1				6	9	5	
6					7	2		
	8	2			4	6		
9		7	6					4
5			2	6	8	4		3
			7	3				
					5	8	2	9

Medium Puzzle 222

DATE: TIME: ~

				4	5			6
7	8	5				2		4
		6	9			7	1	
		9	8				3	
		1	4	2				
			3		1	9	5	2
		8	5					9
	4						2	
			2		7	1		

Medium Puzzle 223

DATE: TIME: ~

8		4	2		6		7	
	6					9	2	4
					9	6	8	
6				7	2	1		
	2		4			5		8
	4	5		1	8			
			8			2		
	5	9						3
	7				1			

Medium Puzzle 224

DATE: TIME: ~

		8			2	5	3	
	4	3	9					6
	6	1			8	2	9	
8	2		1					
							7	2
			5	2	3			8
			6		7	4		
	3			5	1			9
9	5		3				2	7

Medium Puzzle 225

DATE: TIME: ~

8		6		1	3	5		
7			6	9	2			
	9					7		
5				6	8			4
			4		1			3
		9			5			1
	6					8		
2	3		8	5		1	6	
			3			4		

Medium Puzzle 226

DATE: TIME: ~

		4		8				5
1			9			3		7
	6	3			2		8	
4			8			2		
3	7	9						
		5	7		3		4	
			6	4				
	8			7	9	5		
9		7				6	1	

Medium Puzzle 227

DATE: TIME: ~

4	1							7
5		9				8	1	
					6		5	4
3	7		6		1			2
		6						
2	9			3	8	7		
		4	2	8	5	1		
			1	4			2	6
1		7					4	8

Medium Puzzle 228

DATE: TIME: ~

	5			6	2	1		
		2	8	9			6	
		9						2
			2	7	3		8	
2		4					9	3
		1						5
7	4		6	2				
	1		7		4	5		
			3					7

Medium Puzzle 229

DATE: TIME: ~

		1			2	7	9	8
8								
5		7					6	3
		3	8		4	5		
	5		6			9		
4	7	6						1
7				4		6		
9	3	5					1	2
	8		9		1		7	

Medium Puzzle 230

DATE: TIME: ~

						7		
		2		6	9			5
			2			1	6	4
	8		9	2	5		1	
1			3	7	8			9
		9	6				7	8
		7		1		2		
5			8		2			
2	3				6	8		

Medium Puzzle 231

DATE: TIME: ~

1				7			5	
				6		1	8	
7	4	8					9	
	6		3	9	7			
			1	8				9
		1		4	2			5
9			4					
	8				1		2	
6	7			5	8			4

Medium Puzzle 232

DATE: TIME: ~

	3			6	2			
		1	9				6	3
		9	4		1	2		8
7	1	3						6
2				4	7	5	8	
		8			9		2	7
							1	
1	6	5		2				4
				8		7		

Medium Puzzle 233

DATE: TIME: ~

	9					2		4
6	8	4		1	2	5	9	
					4			6
			9			7		8
9	7							
	3	6	1					5
	1	3		4		8		2
8	4				6			
			7	8				3

Medium Puzzle 234

DATE: TIME: ~

		7				9		
				6			2	
5	2					3		1
4		9		2	1		7	
	1		5	7				
3			8	9	4			
	5	8	4			1		2
9				1		6		
1	6		2				4	

Medium Puzzle 235

DATE: TIME: ~

9	8						4	
5	7		2	4	3		8	
	1			9				7
8				6			9	2
3								4
		7		5	4		6	
			4				7	
		8				3		1
6			1	3			2	8

Medium Puzzle 236

DATE: TIME: ~

7			5		3			4
4	1	5	7			2	3	9
3		8	2				6	5
6				2			9	
	7		3			4		
					5			6
	5			8	2		7	
						6		
	6	3			7	8		

Medium Puzzle 237

DATE: TIME: ~

2	5							
1			2					
	8	4			6		2	
		7		5	2	8		3
4	2	5	3		1	7	9	
						5		
	1						6	
5			1	4	9			7
7		3				9	8	

Medium Puzzle 238

DATE: TIME: ~

1	3		4			7	6	
		4				2	3	
	2			9	3	5		
					7	3		
					6		8	2
6			3	4			7	
					4	1	2	
		2	6		9		4	
	5	3	2					

Medium Puzzle 239

DATE: TIME: ~

2			1	6	4	7		
			5			1		8
	1						6	
		6	7	3				
3	5	7	2				9	6
		1		4		8		
	7	8				6	4	
		2		5				3
4				2			7	

Medium Puzzle 240

DATE: TIME: ~

7	8							
	3	9			6			
		4	7				1	3
	1				3		7	
4			9			3		
	5		6	4		2		
2	4				8		6	
8	6			7	9	4	2	5
					2	8	3	

Medium Puzzle 241

DATE: TIME: ~

					3		2	
8	7							1
3		2	8	9	1			
	4				5			2
5	3	8			6		7	
2				4		3		5
		5		3		2	6	7
	2			6	9		5	
6		1		5				3

Medium Puzzle 242

DATE: TIME: ~

	6		9	1		2		4
4					6			8
			4	7		3		
7				9			4	
	4		7		5		1	2
	9	5				8	3	
		2		4	7	6	8	9
9		8	6				5	
	3							

Medium Puzzle 243

DATE: TIME: ~

5	6	4			3			
7			4	2				
	9				1	5		
				7				8
	4				9		6	7
3		8	5				4	2
						7	1	6
	3			5				
8		9	6		7		3	5

Medium Puzzle 244

DATE: TIME: ~

4		3	2		5	8	1	
5		1						
	7			1	9	3		5
	1							2
			7	9			3	
9	6			2	8		5	7
	4	2			6			
8			5		2			
	5			8		2		

Medium Puzzle 245

DATE: TIME: ~

4							9	1
	3				6	5		2
	1			8	9		3	
5		8	1		3	2		
1			6				5	
2				5			1	8
	5		8				2	9
		7		3	2			
		1			7		6	

Medium Puzzle 246

DATE: TIME: ~

	6		3		8		4	
	7	4			5			
				9				
			6			9	3	
3		1		7		4		6
	4		5	3				
7		6		5	1			4
2							8	7
				8	3	2		1

Medium Puzzle 247

DATE: TIME: ~

3		6			9		2	
	9	8			3			6
			1					8
8			7	5			6	9
	5	9						
			9	8				2
		3		9		8	5	
			4	1	5		9	
		5	3	6			4	

Medium Puzzle 248

DATE: TIME: ~

7	6		1		3	4		
4					8	6		
2	5			6	9	3		
		5	6					
				9		8	7	
1			3					
		6			2	1	9	5
	8		7			2		3
5		1				7		8

Medium Puzzle 249

DATE: TIME: ~

							7	6
3			4			8	5	
	6	4			2		1	
1		7			6			3
5			7	1				
		9				7	4	
		6		5			3	4
4	1	3	9		8			
		5	6				8	

Medium Puzzle 250

DATE: TIME: ~

			8	7		5	4	
	7			4				
			3	1		6	9	
4	8			6		7	2	3
			7				8	
3	1					9		
	4					2		1
7		1		3		8		5
		5	2		1			

Hard Puzzle 1

DATE: TIME: ~

	7	6			3	2		
2		8		9				
				5		9		
			2					
8	6							
				1	7	3	8	
6		2					4	5
			1					
	1					7		3

Hard Puzzle 2

DATE: TIME: ~

8			7			6	1	
		4	6				3	
1		2						
4						3		
	5				3			4
				1	6			
	2		5		9	4		
5		7					9	
			8					1

Hard Puzzle 3

DATE: TIME: ~

					6			4
7						1	9	
		1		4	3			
	9	3			1			
	2				7		3	
		9		3		2		
		2		5		4		
			4	1			8	5

Hard Puzzle 4

DATE: TIME: ~

3		2					8	
	7		2				3	
		1	5			2		
			8	2				9
				3	4			
						5	7	
8	3					6		
		7			8	4	5	
5				4				

Hard Puzzle 5

DATE: TIME: ~

2						4		
	3						9	
				9		8		
	9				4	2		
1	2			7	5		8	
			1					5
				5		9		2
		1		3		6		
8	5							

Hard Puzzle 6

DATE: TIME: ~

4	8							
		9					6	
6		3	2	9				
	1					4	2	
	5		6				9	8
					4			
		5	1	6				2
7					8		4	
	6			3				

Hard Puzzle 7

DATE: TIME: ~

		6	8			5	3	
9			6					
5						4		
			3		6	7		
		1				3		6
			5					8
		5		1	2			
7	6						4	
		9				8		

Hard Puzzle 8

DATE: TIME: ~

		5	8	4	6	9	7	
	3					4		
	9							1
		8			4		9	
3			2				6	
					8	1		7
	4		1	2				
	5	3	4					
					7			

Hard Puzzle 9

DATE: TIME: ~

								7
		1	3			2		
2	5				6			
		9			4		6	
	7			9		3	1	
5						7		
6		2	1					4
		5						
	4		9	2			7	

Hard Puzzle 10

DATE: TIME: ~

			4			9		3
		3		5	6		1	
1	6		2					
7	2	5	1		4			
		4					3	
	8							
			6		7			
	4		3	8				
		6					2	8

Hard Puzzle 11

DATE: TIME: ~

					5	8		9
							5	
			6	2				1
8	9					3	7	
	3	6	8			2		
7			9	5				6
		3		7	2			
	6							
	4			6			3	

Hard Puzzle 12

DATE: TIME: ~

8	4			1		2	7	
	2		6				8	
		6						
6						9		
			1		4			
	8	5		9				
9				4				1
		7	3		6			4
4								

Hard Puzzle 13

DATE: TIME: ~

	5	7	8			6		
				9		8		
	3			4				
			5			2		
6		8		1				7
		5					3	
4			2		6			
	1				9			
				7	4	9	2	

Hard Puzzle 14

DATE: TIME: ~

		5			8		9	
7	2					6		5
			1					
	9			7				8
			8	3			7	6
			2					
8	4	2						7
					7	5		
3				1				

Hard Puzzle 15

DATE: TIME: ~

	3	7		4	8	6		
			3	6	2			5
6							8	
	4			3			2	7
	1						6	
		5			3		1	
			8		5			
9			7	2		8		

Hard Puzzle 16

DATE: TIME: ~

					6		5	8
2			9	4				
	5		3		1			
		5			3			6
1						8		4
	4			6		1	9	
			5			3		
	8					4		2
4								

Hard Puzzle 17

DATE: TIME: ~

	5		9			4		
				1				
	9	6	8					2
8					5			6
7								
	2					3	9	
2	4				9	1	7	
	6			2	3			
							2	3

Hard Puzzle 18

DATE: TIME: ~

3				5				2
				1				
4		7	8					
		2				3		6
	1		2	9		8		
5								
		3					8	
6			4				7	
						6	4	1

Hard Puzzle 19

DATE: TIME: ~

		1						7
2								3
				3		4		
			2					
		5		8				6
	9		3	6		8		4
				9				
	7				4		1	
6	3		8					

Hard Puzzle 20

DATE: TIME: ~

7		5	6			8		
				1			7	
2			3					
3	9							
	1	2						5
	4		9	7				2
			2				4	
		8						1
		3			6			7

Hard Puzzle 21

DATE: TIME: ~

		3	5		6			8
9				2		4		7
	8	7						3
			6			7	3	4
			7				9	
8				9				6
			4					
2				5	9			
					2			

Hard Puzzle 22

DATE: TIME: ~

				2				5
3		2			6			
	9		8		7			6
5		1					7	
				9				
					4	1	2	
7		4			9			
	2	8			3			4
6								

Hard Puzzle23

DATE: TIME: ~

			6		3	8		
		1		7				
9						1		2
	5			9				
4				8		6		
					6			
6		8	9		7	3		
	3				2		9	
					8		5	

Hard Puzzle 24

DATE: TIME: ~

	5				9	4		
			1					
8							6	
			3					
		1		2			5	7
	2	3	9				1	
			2	8	3			
5				1			2	4
1					4	8		

Hard Puzzle 25

DATE: TIME: ~

		1					5	
7			8				2	
	4	8			9			
	6						3	
			4	5		6		
					8	4	1	
	3	4	2		6			
8				9				
	7					3	6	

Hard Puzzle 26

DATE: TIME: ~

		2			6	7		
	3		1					2
9				3			6	
		9		2				
			5			9		1
	7						5	
8			7			1		
				1			8	6
6				9			7	

Hard Puzzle 27

DATE: TIME: ~

						1		
6	3	5						
					8		2	5
					5			
1				2				7
	6					9	8	
2					4			
7							3	6
9			7	3		8		2

Hard Puzzle 28

DATE: TIME: ~

3				6	7			
		5				9		
	2	6		4			3	
7	9	1	6					
	6	8	5		4			1
	5							2
				5	1		7	
			4	8				3
	8							9

Hard Puzzle 29

DATE: TIME: ~

	1					5		6
				5				
3		4			7	1	9	
	6			2		9		
4			9	1				
		8			3			
	9		4		6			3
			7			2		1
							6	

Hard Puzzle 30

DATE: TIME: ~

			6	7				
	3	7				6		
	5							
8		5					1	9
	4	3	1					8
					2			
				5		9		
	9					2	8	
				8	6	4		5

Hard Puzzle 31

DATE: TIME: ~

					8			
	6		1	3			4	
		1			9		3	
	7	4	8			5		
		5		2		6	1	9
				5	2			
8	2	9						7
								6

Hard Puzzle 32

DATE: TIME: ~

			9		1	4		
9			6					3
	5				2	8		
1			2					
		7		8	4			1
						7		5
5	7			6				
	3	9						
6		1					4	

Hard Puzzle 33

DATE: TIME: ~

	3	6		4		5		
	1			6				2
			1			7	4	
		8		5				
			6				2	7
6		7						
2					9			5
			2			1	9	
		5		1				4

Hard Puzzle 34

DATE: TIME: ~

8	6	1				9		
						2		
	9							6
	7			1			8	
				5	9			3
2	4		3					
				7	6			
7		5			1		4	
			8	4				

Hard Puzzle 35

DATE: TIME: ~

2		8		6	9	4		
					2			
				5				
	4	7				5		9
				8			3	
	3			4		6		2
1								7
	2					1	6	3
	5		6	2				

Hard Puzzle 36

DATE: TIME: ~

2		4	8		3			
		9					7	5
				9	6	2		
		3			8			4
5							9	
				2				
	5			6				
		1	5	4	9		2	
		7				9		

Hard Puzzle 37

DATE: TIME: ~

		9	3					
		7		9				4
	4						3	
9							4	
6			1					
	8	2						
	6				9		8	2
5					2			7
	7			8		6	5	

Hard Puzzle 38

DATE: TIME: ~

6	5		7		3			4
	8				2			
			8			7		9
	6	2					3	
						8		
9			6					7
			3				7	2
		4		9	8			3
					4			

Hard Puzzle 39

DATE: TIME: ~

		2					8	
			4			7	3	
		9				5		6
				1				8
			6		8	9	4	
	3							
8				5		3		
7	5			6				
	6		7		1			

Hard Puzzle 40

DATE: TIME: ~

1		2	9					
			2				4	
				8				3
		3			1	5		
		7	8			6		
			5					7
	4			1	2			
	5						7	
2			3	6				1

Hard Puzzle 41

DATE: TIME: ~

		7				5		3
6		1	2					9
			1		7			
				7				
9		3	8		6		7	
						4		2
	4							
			9			2		1
		9			8		3	

Hard Puzzle 42

DATE: TIME: ~

		4				6		
				5	9		8	
								7
				2		5		
9	1	6			3			
	7							8
1				9			5	
	3	2			5			6
8			6				3	

Hard Puzzle 43

DATE: TIME: ~

9				5				8
								2
	3		6	4				
		3	7	6				
	7	5						3
8		4			9			
	1		2		6		5	
		9		7				1
			5		3			

Hard Puzzle 44

DATE: TIME: ~

9	5					7	3	
			9		2	4		
			7					8
	3		6	7				
	8							9
				3			4	
3								6
5		4		2				
		2				8		

Hard Puzzle 45

DATE: TIME: ~

		8					5	
3					1			9
1					9			
	2		9		8			
		7		5		3		1
							6	
9							4	6
	5		4					7
				7				

Hard Puzzle 46

DATE: TIME: ~

		6	4					5
2					5			
		7		9	6			
	4			6			1	
7							3	8
			2		4		9	
	2							
1		3					4	
5	8			2				

Hard Puzzle 47

DATE: TIME: ~

		3		1			9	
								4
		2			6			
1				7	9		4	
6				4				
		9	3		5			2
		4		6				
5		6		3	1			
					7	5	8	

Hard Puzzle 48

DATE: TIME: ~

	3		5	2		1		
9				8	4	7		2
		4	9					5
5	6		2					
8		1		5		3		
3								
				6		4	5	1
				4				6
							7	

Hard Puzzle 49

DATE: TIME: ~

6			5					
	9		1					7
					4	5		8
9				7				
7						2		5
		5	8					
			6	5			2	
			2	3		4		1
			7				9	

Hard Puzzle 50

DATE: TIME: ~

	2	5						4
9				8		5		
		6		3			2	
	4			5			6	8
	7			1	8			
			4				7	
	6							
			9	4		8		3
			5					

Hard Puzzle 51

DATE: TIME: ~

	5			6	9	7		
		4		3			1	
				7		5	4	
8	1		6					4
6							8	
	9			5	2			
9						8		5
					1	3	2	

Hard Puzzle 52

DATE: TIME: ~

2				8	5	3		
7						9		
	1						4	
	4				7	1	5	
9								3
			8					4
6								
		3		1			6	9
	2			9		7		1

Hard Puzzle 53

DATE: TIME: ~

							4	
				6	5	2		
5		8			3			7
	9			1		6		
			8					
	7	4						
	3	7	5		1			
	1		6	4				
6					7			4

Hard Puzzle 54

DATE: TIME: ~

				3				4
			6		7	5		
	3	6			5	8		
9			7					1
		1	8				9	
		8		1		6		
4					6			2
5		7					1	

Hard Puzzle 55

DATE: TIME: ~

3				8	7			
		6				4		
		4	6					3
	8		2				6	9
4						7		5
		1		7				
					9			
6		5	3				4	
				2				7

Hard Puzzle 56

DATE: TIME: ~

			3					6
	4				6	7		9
7		3		8				
		5	7		9	1		
1			2					
		9	4		5			
				2			6	
				9		5	4	
3		8						

Hard Puzzle 57

DATE: TIME: ~

	3				9	2		
8		6						
					2			1
	1				7	6		
5			9	6				7
				5			9	4
	6					3		
		7					8	2
		3					7	

Hard Puzzle 58

DATE: TIME: ~

			1	4			5	
						9	2	
			2	7	9			1
2	7			1				3
		5	4					
3	8							
				2				6
	1	2					8	
6				3				9

Hard Puzzle 59

DATE: TIME: ~

			8	4				9
							4	5
		1			6			
		2						
	7			1	8		5	
	1	3	4		2			8
	3	9			1	4		7
		7	9					2
	6						8	

Hard Puzzle 60

DATE: TIME: ~

	1			2				
5			1					6
4		7				9		
				1				3
					9			
		3	8			5		7
		6				1	3	
	3		7				8	
		8						4

Hard Puzzle 61

DATE: TIME: ~

				3		4	2	
		1				8	7	
		8			2	1		6
		5			6		9	
	6		4	1				
3			5					
	8		6		1			
		9		2			6	7

Hard Puzzle 62

DATE: TIME: ~

9	1						2	
		7						
2			8	1		5		
1					4			
			7				6	
		2		3		7		
	6				9		1	
		3				2		5
			5	8				7

Hard Puzzle 63

DATE: TIME: ~

6						9		
			3				5	
9			2					
		6			4			7
	2						6	
	4		7	9				
7				8		5		1
				1	7			6
			5				2	

Hard Puzzle 64

DATE: TIME: ~

		8					2	
				6			5	7
			8					
6				5			8	
	2					9	3	
		9	2					
8			4			1		
	3	5			6			
7		2			9			

Hard Puzzle 65

DATE: TIME: ~

						7		
	9						5	
2	5		9	3	4			
		4		1		9		
3				9			4	
	6					2		
			6	4				7
	1		2		8			
6		3						

Hard Puzzle 66

DATE: TIME: ~

2						1		
				4			5	
	6		8		1			
	9			7	4			
					9		1	
	8	7					4	
8							2	
		2	7	5				3
		4	3			6		

Hard Puzzle 67

DATE: TIME: ~

			9		3	6		4
			4				1	
	4							
5		2						
3			5			7		8
	8	6	1				5	2
		9		3		8		
2		1			6			
					1		2	

Hard Puzzle 68

DATE: TIME: ~

	3							
	7	6					4	
			4		8		2	
	6				1			
						2	1	
5		7	6	9				
				5				
			3	4		6		
3	4							9

Hard Puzzle 69

DATE: TIME: ~

5		1		6		2		
	3	8						
		2						4
1			9		2	5		3
			7			1		
8	7	6	5				9	
	9		3			7		

Hard Puzzle 70

DATE: TIME: ~

		8						7
			1		6	3		
2	1	5						
	9						6	2
4			6				1	
7		3					8	
8				6	2			
		9			3			
			4	1			9	

Hard Puzzle 71

DATE: TIME: ~

			7	3				
		9						
1						6		7
9			4			3		2
7		6					4	
		8			6			1
4			6	7			2	3
					9	7		4
							8	

Hard Puzzle 72

DATE: TIME: ~

						9		
3				6	8			
6		5	3	9				7
4								
8							5	
			6	1	3			
	4				2			3
	8		5		6	1		2
		2					7	8

Hard Puzzle 73

DATE: TIME: ~

		3	5					
	2			4				
	9	8		3		6		
	7	6		8	1		5	
1	5				9		7	
		1		7	6			
7			2		4			3
						8		

Hard Puzzle 74

DATE: TIME: ~

	4					7		
3				9				
	6		8		2			
		1		8				6
			9	3			8	
			2		7	3		
6			4			1	9	2
	5		3			4		

Hard Puzzle 75

DATE: TIME: ~

5				1			8	3
	2							
	6				3			
1			4	6		2		
							1	
	4			5				7
		7				5		8
		2		9	6			
	9	3		7				2

Hard Puzzle 76

DATE: TIME: ~

		8		4			6	
6				7		5		3
					1		4	
9								2
7	3		2			1		
2			6	5				9
	1			8				
							7	

Hard Puzzle 77

DATE: TIME: ~

			1	8				
2		3	7			4	1	8
7					6			
		4						7
	5					2		
		7			2	3		9
				4				
1					7			
			3	9				5

Hard Puzzle 78

DATE: TIME: ~

	7					1		
5		2					9	4
		4						
					4		5	
	3			7				
		1			9		6	3
			3	2		8	1	
								9
		5	4			7		

Hard Puzzle 79

DATE: TIME: ~

			4	6				3
		9		1				
1	7		3			8		
6					5			4
	1			2				
2	8		7		6			
8			5				3	
					1	6		
9						5	7	

Hard Puzzle 80

DATE: TIME: ~

				7	6			
8	4		5				1	
			2					5
			6	8				2
		6				9		
					7	5		
		3				1		9
	5	7	9				4	
				2	1			

Hard Puzzle 81

DATE: TIME: ~

6		3		8				7
	2	4		3			8	
						5		4
	3			9	5			
9					7		2	
		1	2					5
	4				6			
		7			1	2		

Hard Puzzle 82

DATE: TIME: ~

	2	6			5			
					1	7		
				2		4		
	7							9
		3		6				
2					3			1
		5	1					
7					9	6	4	2
				7		9		

Hard Puzzle 83

DATE: TIME: ~

1								2
	6					9		
9	5				4			
							7	
	8			6	2	3		
		7				6		
		6	3	4			8	
		3		2			1	
				5			9	

Hard Puzzle 84

DATE: TIME: ~

		4					6	
6			2					
	9				3	8		4
4	3	2			1			
	6		4					
				3			5	
	4	9				5		
8			5				1	2
				8				7

Hard Puzzle 85

DATE: TIME: ~

						7	6	
		1		4	6		3	8
5	8			3			9	
				5			7	
			1		2			
		4			8			
			8					
6						5		
		2	3				1	9

Hard Puzzle 86

DATE: TIME: ~

4					9			
6	7			5	3			
2					1	5		9
	8		2	1			4	
		1	3					
								6
			6					
		3		7		9	2	
		2				7		1

Hard Puzzle 87

DATE: TIME: ~

								3
					2	8	1	
			8		6	2		4
				9	7			
	1	4						
5				1			9	
	9							
	4	6	7					2
				3				8

Hard Puzzle 88

DATE: TIME: ~

1				3	7			
7		6				4		
5	2		4					1
	1		2			7	9	
				5				
	4		3					2
			9					
				2	3	5		
			7	8	5	1	2	

Hard Puzzle 89

DATE: TIME: ~

7		3		9		8		
	2	1	3				6	
		2		7	4	9		3
6								
				5		7		
1		9		4				
		4	2					
	5				1		7	

Hard Puzzle 90

DATE: TIME: ~

	5		6					3
	3	2	9					
7	8						4	
				2		4		
					3	8	5	7
			7		9			
4		8			6		1	
	1					3		
	2				1		8	6

Hard Puzzle 91

DATE: TIME: ~

						5		9
2								
			7	3			2	
		5				8	3	
7		2		1				
	1		6		8		9	
			9	2				6
	6						8	
						4		5

Hard Puzzle 92

DATE: TIME: ~

		4					5	
	7				1	3		2
	5			4	9			
				7	2			3
		5				9	1	7
				5				
2		6						
	8		6			4	7	
					4			

Hard Puzzle 93

DATE: TIME: ~

					1	6		
8				9				
	7							3
6			9		3	4		5
3		5		7				8
		9		8		1	2	
4			7					
							4	

Hard Puzzle 94

DATE: TIME: ~

	1	6	9					
		5						4
					7	1		
			2					6
	4				3	8		
7		1		9				
			7	2				
8		2	6		4		3	
				3				9

Hard Puzzle 95

DATE: TIME: ~

				8	7			
		8			5	3		
	3					6	7	
	8				2			
	9		6	1				
7							1	
9					8			4
1				7				
		2	4			5		

Hard Puzzle 96

DATE: TIME: ~

		3		1		4		
8			2		5			
5	1			7			6	
7	5			2				
	8							
2				6			1	
			3				5	
		2						3
			4					9

Hard Puzzle 97

DATE: TIME: ~

					5			
		4			6	3		
	9		2	7				
	7	8		1				9
				5	4	2		
	6		7					
			5					6
8							7	4
	3				9	1		

Hard Puzzle 98

DATE: TIME: ~

		5	8					
	8		1					7
				2	4	3		
	5				7	4	9	
	3					7		
8		2						
			9				1	2
6				4				
				5				

Hard Puzzle 99

DATE: TIME: ~

	2							3
5		7	6					9
		9		1				
	6	3				5		
			7				6	
7			2					4
			8		7			
9							2	
	4	5		9				1

Hard Puzzle 100

DATE: TIME: ~

7					3			
		9			5			
			6	7				4
	1						3	7
						1		8
	6			5		4		
6								
		7				3	2	
	9		4	8				5

Hard Puzzle 101

DATE: TIME: ~

	3	8						
			7			5	1	
			9	6				
2			8	9				
7			6	2	4		3	
	9	5						6
9	1	2		4	3			7
			2			4		

Hard Puzzle 102

DATE: TIME: ~

		5					9	7
			4					
		3			9	8	6	
				5				
	7		9		3			
6	2					5		
				4		9		
		2	6	7				
	8					6	4	1

Hard Puzzle 103

DATE: TIME: ~

							2	4
		4	6			5	1	
				1	2			8
						6		
	8		7		5			
		7			4			9
1								
6					8	4		
	2	5	9		7			

Hard Puzzle 104

DATE: TIME: ~

		8		7	9	5		
2						4		
		3				8		
5	3		4		1			9
	6				3		4	
3			9					7
9								
		2		4	8		6	

Hard Puzzle 105

DATE: TIME: ~

					2	1		
		2	3		5			6
6				8				
								7
3		1	8			9	5	
	5			2		8		
7	4	8						
1					9	4		
9							1	

Hard Puzzle 106

DATE: TIME: ~

5				2	1	4		
	2	1		9	3		7	
		5				1		
			1		5	9		4
			9				8	5
	7			3				
	6	2				7		9
				4				6

Hard Puzzle 107

DATE: TIME: ~

7	1	3		9		8		
							9	
9			6	8				4
	8		2			6		
		2	5		8			
3		4						
		6	3	2				
2					4		6	
			8				3	7

Hard Puzzle 108

DATE: TIME: ~

	6	5	1			3		
4		3		7				
			2				7	
								5
	1	7			3			8
			8		9			3
					1			
	8	1		4			5	
	4			6		2		

Hard Puzzle 109

DATE: TIME: ~

			3					
	1		4			2		
5		7			2			8
7			5			8		
		2		6			7	
				8			6	
		8	9					7
9				3				4
6	5		7					

Hard Puzzle 110

DATE: TIME: ~

1							4	7
					9	2		1
	2	9		7				
2	7				5	1		
			8					9
						8	6	
			9					
3				1				6
7		6	3		4			

Hard Puzzle 111

DATE: TIME: ~

5			3			2		
3	4							
						3		
4								9
1		5	2				3	
	9			1		8		
	8				7			
	1			5	8	6	4	
								2

Hard Puzzle 112

DATE: TIME: ~

	3							
7			9					
6				5				
		9	6			4	2	
5		6			2		8	3
8					9	5		
	5				4			
		1	3				6	
								1

Hard Puzzle 113

DATE: TIME: ~

					2		1	
			4					
	5							9
8		3					7	
2			9			6		
			5				4	8
1						8		
			7		4		9	
	3			6				5

Hard Puzzle 114

DATE: TIME: ~

1			7					
		9					1	
3						9		
					9			
6		4		2				8
8	3	5		6				
	1						7	
		3	2	5		6		
			4				5	2

Hard Puzzle 115

DATE: TIME: ~

								2
4				9				5
		3	7				1	
6	2		3				8	
					5	9		
						1		
	5		2	4	8			
8				6				9
		1				7		

Hard Puzzle 116

DATE: TIME: ~

2			5				7	
6				3			8	
	7	9				1		3
			4	1				
	9			2		7		
		2			8			
								4
8	4						3	9
	3			8			6	

Hard Puzzle 117

DATE: TIME: ~

					8			
8		1			6		5	
9			4				2	
	1				5	7		
	4	6		3				
						8		3
	9		1	8				
	3				7			4
			9		3			

Hard Puzzle 118

DATE: TIME: ~

	2		3			5		7
	3		6		5			
9	8					3		
		9					6	
				7				3
7	1	6						8
		3		1				
								2
	7		5	4				

Hard Puzzle 119

DATE: TIME: ~

				8		7	9	4
		2	3					
	8					9	1	
		1	4		7	5		6
			5					
	5	4		7				
				4				8
7					1			2

Hard Puzzle 120

DATE: TIME: ~

							6	1
5	8	9			4			7
			2	8				4
					3	6		
		2	6	7				
4	9						2	
1				3				
	4							
						9	8	

Hard Puzzle 121

DATE: TIME: ~

	8				1			
					2		6	4
	5	4						
	3		8					
		9	5				1	
			3	7		5		
1			7		5			3
2				9			4	
	7							

Hard Puzzle 122

DATE: TIME: ~

4					6			
	2	7		1			3	
5						4		6
			2					
				9				1
		8		5			9	
9		6			7	3	1	
		3			5		7	
					2			

Hard Puzzle 123

DATE: TIME: ~

	3		2	9				
	2				8	1	3	
							2	4
		6						
			1			4		8
		9	3	4	5			
	4	1					8	
9					6			
3		8				7		2

Hard Puzzle 124

DATE: TIME: ~

4								
				3	2	4	1	8
					1	2		
	8	7						
9		6	8					3
	2			6				
					3			2
	7		5			1		6
			7	8			5	

Hard Puzzle 125

DATE: TIME: ~

			5					
	4			2			1	
				1	7	2	5	
			6		5		3	
3							8	7
	1							
1		7			3			
	2							
		6				9		4

Hard Puzzle 126

DATE: TIME: ~

5					4		6	7
	4							
		1	3	6				8
			9				3	
	7	8	1					9
3				2				
	1				7			
2								
9					6	3		

Hard Puzzle 127

DATE: TIME: ~

5		9		4			3	
6	1				9	7		
8			7		6			
				3				
	4					1		
	6				5			4
			6				1	
1							2	6
	9				7	3		

Hard Puzzle 128

DATE: TIME: ~

2				7		3	8	
4	1		2			9		
		8	9		5		2	
9	3	2			4		6	5
						7	4	
			8					3
	8	3		6				9
		7	5	9			1	8
				8	7	4	3	6

Hard Puzzle 129

DATE: TIME: ~

1			6					8
				5			6	
				2		4		
	9				4	3		
		7		8				
	4	3					9	
					2	9		
	8	5	3				4	
7	2							

Hard Puzzle 130

DATE: TIME: ~

				7				5
8	4					6		
	7	9	8	1			3	
		6	9					
4	8						1	
		2	6			5	4	
			2	6				4
2			1	8	4			

Hard Puzzle 131

DATE: TIME: ~

7				1		3		
3		4						6
	5				7			8
	8			4			6	
		9	7					
5		1			9		3	
	6		2					
				3				
4					5		7	9

Hard Puzzle 132

DATE: TIME: ~

		8	5	4			1	
					1			2
		4			3		9	
4		9						8
1		3	4					
		5			6			
		1		5				9
	4		3			2		
	7					1		

Hard Puzzle 133

DATE: TIME: ~

								6
				3	6	8		
			1			7	9	
	2	6				9		
9				8	5		4	
			6		4			
6								5
	5	8						1
	3		4					

Hard Puzzle 134

DATE: TIME: ~

		8					5	
							7	
	7				5	9		1
7	8		9					6
		1			2			
		5	8			2		3
	3					1	4	
8		9		4				
	1	6		7				

Hard Puzzle 135

DATE: TIME: ~

			9	5	4	3		
2				6				4
	3	6		7		8		
6	5			3				
	8		5	1				
							7	
		2						
		3					6	7
9	7		4					

Hard Puzzle 136

DATE: TIME: ~

2							4	6
				6				8
						1	9	
4		6	7					
	9					3	1	
				2				
		7	3				2	
6	8		4					9
	5		9			8		

Hard Puzzle 137

DATE: TIME: ~

9		1			7			
				1				4
		5				3		
							8	
		4	1		9		5	
2						4		
4			5		2			1
	8							3
		6			3		4	7

Hard Puzzle 138

DATE: TIME: ~

	7		2					
					5			
	4			9	6			
8				3		9		
		3		4				
			7				4	
1			5				6	
		8				4	7	
		6	3					2

Hard Puzzle 139

DATE: TIME: ~

						1		2
	3				8			7
			4	7				
	2							6
		8		5	3			
							7	
7	8	2					5	
		4			6		9	
9			2					1

Hard Puzzle 140

DATE: TIME: ~

		4				6	8	7
2		5						
					7		3	
	6					1		8
4		7	9					
			5					
								5
1		2	8					
9				2		4		6

Hard Puzzle 141

DATE: TIME: ~

					9	3		5
		1					7	
9	8			5				
4			1	3	5	9		
		5			8			
						6		7
7	5			6				
		4					3	
				4			2	

Hard Puzzle 142

DATE: TIME: ~

	3	4					7	2
6		2	3			4		
		3			1	8		9
	8	9	4			3		
1				9	6			3
	5	6		3				
				7			2	

Hard Puzzle 143

DATE: TIME: ~

	7					1		
2		3	5					
			8		6	3		
								7
	5		4		8		9	
	6	4	1					3
7						9		
							8	
8		9	3	1				

Hard Puzzle 144

DATE: TIME: ~

9		3	5				4	
	4							6
			1		9			7
3	5							
		4		6				
						2		
4				7			6	
			9					
	8	7				9	1	

Hard Puzzle 145

DATE: TIME: ~

				7				
			6				5	
1	4				8	3		
			5	3				
					7			9
	6		9				2	
6	2				4	5	9	
3		1				2		
5				6			8	

Hard Puzzle 146

DATE: TIME: ~

7					8			
		1		2				
3			6					2
		3		9				7
	7				4			
		2	8	1		4		
6	9	4			1			
		8					4	
				6	9			

Hard Puzzle 147

DATE: TIME: ~

		6	3					9
		1	9	6		5		
3					1			
			8			6		4
		3				9		
	2						7	
6		5						
				9	7			2
2			5			8		

Hard Puzzle 148

DATE: TIME: ~

2					9		5	
					5	1		7
		1		8		2		
	6			3				2
3			6	4				
	7							
		3	2			5		4
								8
4		9	3					

Hard Puzzle 149

DATE: TIME: ~

	3							
				5	2			1
4			1	7				9
			4		7	1		
	4	8		2				
		5	6		8			
						3		
		6			1	9		7
7						8		4

Hard Puzzle 150

DATE: TIME: ~

	9		7	6			3	
						9		1
		2		5			4	
					1			8
		4				3	7	
	2	6						4
	4			3	6			
				2		1		
	5				8		2	

Hard Puzzle 151

DATE: TIME: ~

6				8			4	5
		9						
	7				4	9		
		8					3	6
					1	7	5	
5	4							
1		6	9					
					3	2		
			6					9

Hard Puzzle 152

DATE: TIME: ~

		1		7				4
							3	8
	9	5			3			
		6			5			2
9								7
		2			6		9	
		3		5		1		
	4		3		2		8	9
				6				

Hard Puzzle 153

DATE: TIME: ~

3	9							1
			2					
6					1	2		4
		1			2		6	
			5		3	4		
				4			8	
2				6				
9		8						
					4		7	6

Hard Puzzle 154

DATE: TIME: ~

4		1			5			6
9			7	2				8
		5	8				9	4
	3				9			
					6	5		
7				8				
	2						1	
		4	1				6	7

Hard Puzzle 155

DATE: TIME: ~

					2			
	3	2		4				
						9	8	
6	8		9		5			
					4	3		6
	5							
	6		7					
		7			1		9	3
		4		8		2		

Hard Puzzle 156

DATE: TIME: ~

		3					1	
						3		4
5	6			1				9
					5			
		9						3
			4	7			2	
9				4				7
		4			2			
	7				8	6		1

Hard Puzzle 157

DATE: TIME: ~

		5				2		
4					6		7	
				8	5			1
5		2		4				3
	1			6				
						5	9	
6					2			8
		1				4		
	8				4		6	9

Hard Puzzle 158

DATE: TIME: ~

						4		3
		9			4	7		
				2	7			5
6			4		8			
		3	1					4
	1					6	9	
5	9		3	1				
4								1
2								

Hard Puzzle 159

DATE: TIME: ~

	3			9			2	
	4							
		9		1		3		
		6				9		5
			4			7		
1		5					8	
			5		8		1	2
		8						
				7				6

Hard Puzzle 160

DATE: TIME: ~

		5		8		1		
6	7		4		5			
	5		7	9				
	2			3			8	
					6			4
		8		6		5		2
		9		4			3	
			2					

Hard Puzzle 161

DATE: TIME: ~

9				4			7	
		5			3			
	7		1		9			
			7			5		9
	8			3			6	
			9	6	2	7		
		2		5				
	4				1	8		
			6			2		5

Hard Puzzle 162

DATE: TIME: ~

					4			
		2			5			1
		7		1	6	5	8	
	6			8				
				3	7	1		4
		1			9			7
		9	5	4	8		1	
			7			9		
				9	1			

Hard Puzzle 163

DATE: TIME: ~

		5	7	4		8		
			9					
7				6			9	2
						1		
6	9	8					7	
5				8		6		
1	4							5
					2		1	
	7		5		4			

Hard Puzzle 164

DATE: TIME: ~

		7	8		5	2		
	8	6				3		
2				4				
	7				3			
4		2						
9			1	2		4		
						8		4
	9	4						6
5				1			2	

Hard Puzzle 165

DATE: TIME: ~

8							4	
					5			
		3	2				6	7
		5			7			
	4			3	8			
9	8						5	
5					3			
	2			6			8	4
		7				2		

Hard Puzzle 166

DATE: TIME: ~

3	8			6				
					7		9	
		2				3		
		5	3		2			
				7			1	9
6						7		5
5	4		7					
9								8
		7				6		

Hard Puzzle 167

DATE: TIME: ~

				2				
		3	1			5		6
	1	7						9
			6		5			
	9	8					4	
			7				8	
			5	7		4	1	
		2	8		3			
	8						6	

Hard Puzzle 168

DATE: TIME: ~

		9	4					3
		7						
2			3				5	
6	1						3	
	9				6		2	
5			7		3			4
		5			8			
				5		8		
	4					7	9	

Hard Puzzle 169

DATE: TIME: ~

6								5
					8			4
2					6	9		
	4		6			2	1	
				9	3			
			2			5	4	
				4		8		2
1	2	8						
	3					6		

Hard Puzzle 170

DATE: TIME: ~

		4	8					1
				2	7		5	
5	7		3					6
7							6	
	1				5		8	
	9		6					
			5				1	
		2	4		1	7		
				3		8		

Hard Puzzle 171

DATE: TIME: ~

				3		4		
	6	3		9				
4		8		2				1
		4					8	2
			7		5			
				1		9	7	
					9			
	1						5	
3						1	6	

Hard Puzzle 172

DATE: TIME: ~

3					1			
4						5	6	
	8		9	5				
	1						3	6
	9						1	
		2			4			
				9				
		6	7					
7			4				5	2

Hard Puzzle 173

DATE: TIME: ~

6			2	3			7	5
	1					9		
	2			7	4			
2		8						
					7			3
	4			6	9	8		
		5						
	7			4		6	9	

Hard Puzzle 174

DATE: TIME: ~

		8	4			6		7
4	3							
		6	5		9			
			2	3				6
		7				5		
1	8						4	
	2					7	8	
				1	8			
		5				1		

Hard Puzzle 175

DATE: TIME: ~

4			5			7		
	9	8					2	
5		3	9			8		1
					5			
							8	
			4	8	2	3		
						9		
2	6				3		7	
7		9						4

Hard Puzzle 176

DATE: TIME: ~

2		5			1			8
	9				8	3		
		4						
							9	
	2			9	7			1
					3	5		
8				7			1	4
					5	7		
	4		6				2	

Hard Puzzle 177

DATE: TIME: ~

	3				1	5		4
	4		3	2	7		1	
9		1	5					
		8		5			2	
	5			6				
			4					
5			2	7		8		1
	7	6			8			
						3		

Hard Puzzle 178

DATE: TIME: ~

	5			7		4		
			4		1		5	
		4	2					
		7					3	
1					3	2		
9						1		
		1		3	8		2	
		8		9				5
	4	3	6		2			

Hard Puzzle 179

DATE: TIME: ~

	9	5		3		4		
				1		8		2
	3			6			1	
9					8			
		2			5	9		3
	8				6		3	
		4				7	5	
			7					

Hard Puzzle 180

DATE: TIME: ~

4	9			2			8	
		3			7			
				9				2
9							2	6
		6						
2		7		8			1	
			6	3	4			
			9			4		
		1		7				

Hard Puzzle 181

DATE: TIME: ~

	1	7	9					
					4	1		
8					7		5	9
			3	1				
7		6						3
	3				5	4		6
		1		4		3		
				9				
	6			5			9	8

Hard Puzzle 182

DATE: TIME: ~

		9		7				5
				3	6			
	3					1		9
	7	3					4	
		1				3		
4							8	
9			6				5	
					5			
1					9	8		2

Hard Puzzle 183

DATE: TIME: ~

				7	1			
4	3				8			9
							4	6
	7		3	4		1		
	5		6					2
	8		7		9	3	6	
3	1	9		2				
						2		

Hard Puzzle 184

DATE: TIME: ~

			8		7		6	
6						1		
	7			6				3
			3		4			2
	5	3						
			2					5
9					5			8
8		1			6			
	4		7				9	

Hard Puzzle 185

DATE: TIME: ~

						5	4	
		1			9		8	
	9			7				
4			7	5				
		2					7	4
				6				
	3		8			9		1
		5	9				2	8
	1		3					

Hard Puzzle 186

DATE: TIME: ~

		4					6	
6			2					
	9				3	8		4
4	3	2			1			
	6		4					
				3			5	
	4	9				5		
8			5				1	2
				8				7

Hard Puzzle 187

DATE: TIME: ~

		6				2	5	8
		4			2			
								9
8		7	6					
2			7			5		
	1				8		6	
	7	2		6				4
				8			2	
1	5						7	

Hard Puzzle 188

DATE: TIME: ~

1			2					
	6		3			8		
8		9				2	3	
	7					5	4	
	4		6	7				
6								3
				5				8
		5	8	6		1		9
						6		

Hard Puzzle 189

DATE: TIME: ~

2		4			7			3
						1		
			6				8	7
7					5	2		9
9		6				4		1
3								
				4			7	
		8	1					
					9			4

Hard Puzzle 190

DATE: TIME: ~

	2	8	9				3	
			7					
					4	8		
	5			9	6	4		
2		6						
		3					5	
9			8		2			
								7
8				4	5			3

Hard Puzzle 191

DATE: TIME: ~

							3	
	7	9						
3			8					2
	5				7		8	1
7	2	8		6		4	9	
	6	4						
					9			
	4		5					3
			7		6	1		

Hard Puzzle 192

DATE: TIME: ~

			5					
5		4		1			2	
				7		8	3	
9			3					8
	7			6		5		
	8	3						2
	9	2		5				
					1		5	6
7								

Hard Puzzle 193

DATE: TIME: ~

		7				3		
				4			8	
		4	2		1		7	
					3	2		5
9								1
	1	3		8				
	8			6				
			4				5	2
		6		7				

Hard Puzzle 194

DATE: TIME: ~

9	7		3		4			
				9				
			8	6			4	
2						7	5	
5		9			6		3	
	3			1	9			
4				8				
		1						8
7		8			5			

Hard Puzzle 195

DATE: TIME: ~

					5		9	
4		6	9			1		
	1		3			2		
	2					4		
7					4			5
	6							
	3							8
	4		8	7	6	3		
				3			1	

Hard Puzzle 196

DATE: TIME: ~

		9		5				
		6				9	3	
7					2		6	
6		7						
3		1	4			2		
				9		1		
	8	3		6	1			
		2		7	3			8

Hard Puzzle 197

DATE: TIME: ~

8			2	3			9	
9								5
	2	4					8	
			6				4	
		6			4		5	
	5				9	3		
			8	2	5	1		
3								4
							6	

Hard Puzzle 198

DATE: TIME: ~

			5		9			
							6	
9		7						4
	3					9		
	8		2	4		7		
4				5		2		
				1	4			
7	6	5		9				
			7				2	

Hard Puzzle 199

DATE: TIME: ~

			9		5	2		
		9	2	4				8
				1				
2						1	5	
4	7					3		
	5			6	1			
		2	5			8		
3	1					5	4	

Hard Puzzle 200

DATE: TIME: ~

6							7	1
	8				1			
				9		6		
4		7	1				8	
8	5		6	2				3
					3	4		
1	3							
		2	4			9		

Hard Puzzle 201

DATE: TIME: ~

		8						
	1							2
	7		5	1				
		6			2			1
		1	7			3		
4	9				1			
				8		2	1	4
7								6
				3	4		7	

Hard Puzzle 202

DATE: TIME: ~

		1	9			3	7	
	3		6	1			2	
		2						5
			3		6	5		
								8
			8				9	1
				5	9		1	4
4								
5						7		

Hard Puzzle 203

DATE: TIME: ~

					2	5		
			4	8				
								7
		6		7	4			
2		7						9
3	9		2					
1					5		8	
		8			1	6	2	
5				3				

Hard Puzzle 204

DATE: TIME: ~

							2	3
		8				7		
6					8			4
		3				9		
	5			7				
4				3	1			
8			5		7			
		2					7	
	1				4		6	

Hard Puzzle 205

DATE: TIME: ~

		5		2				
		3				6		
				5	6			
		2				4		
	4		2	8				1
1			9			7		
							6	
9					4			2
4	2		3			1	9	

Hard Puzzle 206

DATE: TIME: ~

9	3		2					
		5				8		
	6			3			4	7
1	2							
7	5							6
	8			7				3
			7	2				8
4			1	8			9	

Hard Puzzle 207

DATE: TIME: ~

	8				6			5
6			4				1	
		3		7	9			
			9		3			4
			6	8				
					7	3	8	
5	9							
3	6	7				8		
							2	

Hard Puzzle 208

DATE: TIME: ~

							4	
			7	8				
			6		2			9
	8	1				3		2
	3						9	
				3	1			7
1								
		5		4		2		
		2	8		6			1

Hard Puzzle 209

DATE: TIME: ~

			6	7				
	3	7				6		
	5							
8		5					1	9
	4	3	1					8
					2			
				5		9		
	9					2	8	
				8	6	4		5

Hard Puzzle 210

DATE: TIME: ~

	5	2				7	4	
				3				
4				6		8	9	
	7				8			9
							3	
		5		4	1		6	
7		1		9				
	9		6	5				
					4			

Hard Puzzle 211

DATE: TIME: ~

		9				2		
	7					1		
		6		7			8	3
8	5					9		
				5	8			7
				1				
	6		3					
4					2		9	5
	8			6			1	

Hard Puzzle 212

DATE: TIME: ~

		9	1					
							8	7
5				6	9		1	
6						2	5	8
		8	6	3				4
3				7				
8	1					6		2
	2			4				

Hard Puzzle 213

DATE: TIME: ~

	8							
		2		9				
1	9			7			4	
6						2	9	
		7						4
	2	4			8	3		
			9	3				
	5		2	4		8		
			1				2	3

Hard Puzzle 214

DATE: TIME: ~

8	6				7			
4			6			8		
5		3					2	
	5	1			8			
7			1					
			3	4				
						6	8	5
	8				2		3	1
				1				9

Hard Puzzle 215

DATE: TIME: ~

1				8	6			
3				4		8		
6					2			3
5	9							2
					5	7	3	
		3					1	
		4				2		
	5		1					8
7			4	2				

Hard Puzzle 216

DATE: TIME: ~

	6		2		1			3
	2		3	7	5			
	8	7		9	4			
								2
				5			8	
4	5		7			6		1
	9							
				4		7		

Hard Puzzle 217

DATE: TIME: ~

			6				4	
2								
6					9	2		7
8				3		7	6	
	4						3	
				7				1
	1				7	9		8
7	5				6			4
			4			1		

Hard Puzzle 218

DATE: TIME: ~

			2					1
1		9	5					
3							7	
	3				1		8	
	5		4					7
6		7			8		1	
				2				
	8	4		7			6	2
			3		5			

Hard Puzzle 219

DATE: TIME: ~

4		2	1					
5					7			
		1	9					2
				7			2	
7	6		5			4		8
		3				6		
				3			7	
			4		9		8	
3						2	4	

Hard Puzzle 220

DATE: TIME: ~

	5	8			3			
		9		6			7	8
7	4							
							4	9
		5		2				
8								3
		6	4				1	5
		4	9	1		8		
1								7

Hard Puzzle 221

DATE: TIME: ~

9			1	2				
			5		9	8		
1			6			4		
	5	1			6	7		9
							8	1
4					8	5		
	9							7
					5		6	
						3		

Hard Puzzle 222

DATE: TIME: ~

7		5	8			6	4	
			6			5		
	2	3						
		6	4	7			3	
4				2				1
	9						1	
						3	9	
2	4				1		6	

Hard Puzzle 223

DATE: TIME: ~

	5							4
				7	8		6	
6			9					
	9			5		4		
		7						
			2	9				3
8				6		5		9
	7	1		3				
	2				1		4	

Hard Puzzle 224

DATE: TIME: ~

6	5		4				8	
	8				3			9
	1	4		6		7		
			2		9			
7	2				5			1
5				1				
	6				2		1	
			3					2
						5		

Hard Puzzle 225

DATE: TIME: ~

	7					5		
	6	2				4		
9	8							3
3				5	2			
	4		6	3		1	9	
		8	1					
			9		1			
		9	5	7				2
4								

Hard Puzzle 226

DATE: TIME: ~

	2			3	8			
6			9					
			7	2			4	
						7		
8	9							6
4		6						3
	1			9		4		8
2		5	3	4				7

Hard Puzzle 227

DATE: TIME: ~

9			7			2		
	7		4	1				8
2					3			
					8		9	
7		4	3					
			2	4		3		
		3			6		5	
1				9				
8			5		4			

Hard Puzzle 228

DATE: TIME: ~

	3							5
4					6		3	9
			7					
8				9			1	
					2	5		
	2	1			7			
9		8						
			6	1			8	
		6	2	4				

Hard Puzzle 229

DATE: TIME: ~

			1			7		
8						9		
4		2		3		1		
9					6		2	
	3			4				
			8		9			
1		3					5	
	7			9			8	6
				2				

Hard Puzzle 230

DATE: TIME: ~

	4			7				9
		5						
3	8							
							2	
2			9		5		3	
		1		4				7
			8			2	6	
	7				4	8		
				2		3		5

Hard Puzzle 231

DATE: TIME: ~

	7	2			4			
1					6			
8			1				3	
7		4			5			
	8			9		3		
2			6					7
					2		6	
			7				4	
	5			8			9	

Hard Puzzle 232

DATE: TIME: ~

	3		5	2		1		
9				8	4	7		2
		4	9					5
5	6		2					
8		1		5		3		
3								
				6		4	5	1
				4				6
							7	

Hard Puzzle 233

DATE: TIME: ~

7		1					2	
	6		8					
	2				3	5		
			4		8			
	1			3			9	
				2		7		4
					4			
8		3		7				1
	5	7			6	8		

Hard Puzzle 234

DATE: TIME: ~

		1		7		6		
8	4						9	
			5					8
		8	4				3	1
	3	6		2				
								2
9				6	8		4	
		7				2		
								3

Hard Puzzle 235

DATE: TIME: ~

	6			5			3	8
4								
		7	9		8			
				4	1			
	5	2			9			
	9		7	8				
7						4		
		3	2			8		
			4			6	1	

Hard Puzzle 236

DATE: TIME: ~

				1		9		3
					8	6		
4		8		3				
								1
8		6	7					
3		7		2	9			4
	4		9	7		5		
						7		
		3			5			

Hard Puzzle 237

DATE: TIME: ~

3		7				9		
						2		
4			8				3	
	4			8				7
6								
	8	9	4		1		5	
2		1		7				
	3		1		4			
			9	5			6	

Hard Puzzle 238

DATE: TIME: ~

5							9	
		3			7	2		
	8			2				4
6	4				3			
			7	1		4		
	2				8	6		
	5					3		
			9	7				
		4			2	7		

Hard Puzzle 239

DATE: TIME: ~

			4	5				
					8		1	4
7		3					5	
			6				9	1
8								2
		1			9	3		
	5	2						
			5			4		8
	7			2				

Hard Puzzle 240

DATE: TIME: ~

	4		9			2		
				3			7	
6	7				1	8	3	
	1	4		2				
								4
	6	5				9	2	
3			4			6		8
	8		6				5	
			7			3		

Hard Puzzle 241

DATE: TIME: ~

					2			
	3	2		4				
						9	8	
6	8		9		5			
					4	3		6
	5							
	6		7					
		7			1		9	3
		4		8		2		

Hard Puzzle 242

DATE: TIME: ~

	4	8						
1		5		3		9		
	6							4
		3			6			1
6				2			3	
				4				
				6	1			2
2				5		8		
5	7				3		9	

Hard Puzzle 243

DATE: TIME: ~

	4	5	3					
		9	2				8	3
		6						
			1	6				
				5		9	4	
6			9			5	3	
		3			8			
			5	3	2		1	
								9

Hard Puzzle 244

DATE: TIME: ~

	5		3					
		4			2	1		7
8								6
	6		8		4			
						6		1
		5					8	9
	3			9				
9	2			4				
		8	6		7			

Hard Puzzle 245

DATE: TIME: ~

			1			4		
4				6				
5	3		2					8
	1					8	6	3
3		8		9				7
	4							
6		7					1	
			6			9		
						3		

Hard Puzzle 246

DATE: TIME: ~

			4					
		4	9		2			8
	5	8					6	
8		3	1			9	2	
	4							
	6		8	4		7		
9				2		6		
						5	3	
				1				7

Hard Puzzle 247

DATE: TIME: ~

4		1	2					5
						7	4	
		3			1		6	
9				1		8	7	6
	3							
			6	8				
8	9	4						
					3			
			1		5			

Hard Puzzle 248

DATE: TIME: ~

		2		1			9	
3							5	
8				2				4
				3	5			
	5					6		9
				9			1	
9			1			7	4	
		5	2	6				
		7				8		

Hard Puzzle 249

DATE: TIME: ~

						5		9
2								
			7	3			2	
		5				8	3	
7		2		1				
	1		6		8		9	
			9	2				6
	6						8	
						4		5

Hard Puzzle 250

DATE: TIME: ~

	6			8			7	5
					9			
				2		4		
3							6	2
	5	6			8			
		4		9				
4					7		1	6
	2				4			8
					5		4	

Medium Puzzle 1

9	7	5	2	1	3	8	6	4
3	2	4	6	8	9	7	1	5
8	1	6	7	5	4	3	2	9
6	9	2	5	7	8	4	3	1
5	4	1	3	2	6	9	8	7
7	8	3	4	9	1	2	5	6
1	3	7	9	6	2	5	4	8
2	6	9	8	4	5	1	7	3
4	5	8	1	3	7	6	9	2

Medium Puzzle 2

2	4	9	5	1	7	6	3	8
5	7	1	6	3	8	9	2	4
6	3	8	2	9	4	5	7	1
7	8	3	9	5	2	4	1	6
9	2	6	4	7	1	3	8	5
1	5	4	3	8	6	2	9	7
3	9	7	1	6	5	8	4	2
8	6	2	7	4	3	1	5	9
4	1	5	8	2	9	7	6	3

Medium Puzzle 3

9	5	6	8	1	3	2	4	7
4	1	2	9	7	6	5	8	3
3	7	8	2	4	5	9	1	6
7	6	9	3	8	4	1	2	5
5	8	1	7	2	9	3	6	4
2	3	4	6	5	1	7	9	8
6	2	5	4	9	7	8	3	1
8	4	7	1	3	2	6	5	9
1	9	3	5	6	8	4	7	2

Medium Puzzle 4

4	3	7	6	8	2	9	5	1
5	9	1	7	4	3	8	2	6
2	8	6	1	9	5	7	4	3
7	1	4	2	3	8	6	9	5
9	5	2	4	6	1	3	7	8
8	6	3	9	5	7	4	1	2
3	2	5	8	7	9	1	6	4
1	4	9	3	2	6	5	8	7
6	7	8	5	1	4	2	3	9

Medium Puzzle 5

8	4	3	5	7	2	9	1	6
9	2	6	3	1	8	5	4	7
7	1	5	6	9	4	3	2	8
1	6	9	2	4	7	8	3	5
3	7	8	1	5	6	2	9	4
2	5	4	9	8	3	7	6	1
4	3	2	8	6	5	1	7	9
6	8	1	7	2	9	4	5	3
5	9	7	4	3	1	6	8	2

Medium Puzzle 6

5	6	9	2	3	7	8	1	4
3	8	4	9	6	1	7	2	5
7	1	2	8	4	5	3	6	9
6	5	7	3	1	2	4	9	8
2	9	1	4	7	8	6	5	3
4	3	8	5	9	6	2	7	1
1	4	5	6	2	3	9	8	7
8	2	3	7	5	9	1	4	6
9	7	6	1	8	4	5	3	2

Medium Puzzle 7

9	2	5	7	8	4	6	3	1
7	3	4	6	1	5	2	8	9
6	1	8	3	9	2	5	7	4
2	8	6	9	3	1	7	4	5
4	7	1	5	2	6	3	9	8
3	5	9	8	4	7	1	2	6
5	9	7	4	6	3	8	1	2
8	6	2	1	7	9	4	5	3
1	4	3	2	5	8	9	6	7

Medium Puzzle 8

3	9	8	1	5	4	6	2	7
1	5	7	2	6	3	4	8	9
6	2	4	7	8	9	5	1	3
4	6	3	8	1	7	2	9	5
8	7	9	5	4	2	1	3	6
5	1	2	3	9	6	8	7	4
9	8	6	4	3	1	7	5	2
2	3	1	6	7	5	9	4	8
7	4	5	9	2	8	3	6	1

Medium Puzzle 9

5	8	4	3	7	6	2	1	9
2	3	9	4	8	1	6	7	5
7	6	1	9	5	2	3	4	8
3	5	2	8	6	7	4	9	1
1	9	6	5	3	4	7	8	2
4	7	8	2	1	9	5	6	3
9	1	5	6	4	3	8	2	7
8	4	7	1	2	5	9	3	6
6	2	3	7	9	8	1	5	4

Medium Puzzle 10

5	3	1	9	6	7	2	4	8
8	6	4	5	3	2	1	7	9
2	7	9	4	1	8	6	3	5
7	1	6	2	5	9	3	8	4
9	8	2	7	4	3	5	6	1
4	5	3	6	8	1	7	9	2
1	4	5	8	7	6	9	2	3
3	9	7	1	2	4	8	5	6
6	2	8	3	9	5	4	1	7

Medium Puzzle 11

2	8	4	6	1	9	3	5	7
1	6	5	4	7	3	2	8	9
3	9	7	5	2	8	6	4	1
9	3	8	1	6	5	4	7	2
4	5	1	2	8	7	9	6	3
6	7	2	3	9	4	5	1	8
7	1	3	9	4	6	8	2	5
5	2	6	8	3	1	7	9	4
8	4	9	7	5	2	1	3	6

Medium Puzzle 12

5	4	7	3	2	9	6	8	1
8	2	9	4	6	1	3	7	5
3	6	1	8	7	5	9	2	4
9	5	2	6	8	7	4	1	3
7	8	4	9	1	3	5	6	2
1	3	6	2	5	4	7	9	8
2	7	3	5	9	8	1	4	6
4	1	8	7	3	6	2	5	9
6	9	5	1	4	2	8	3	7

Medium Puzzle 13

1	9	4	6	7	5	8	3	2
6	8	5	4	3	2	1	9	7
2	7	3	9	8	1	6	5	4
9	6	7	1	4	8	5	2	3
4	5	8	3	2	7	9	1	6
3	2	1	5	6	9	4	7	8
8	1	2	7	9	6	3	4	5
7	4	9	8	5	3	2	6	1
5	3	6	2	1	4	7	8	9

Medium Puzzle 14

5	9	1	3	2	6	7	4	8
7	8	4	9	1	5	6	2	3
6	2	3	8	7	4	1	9	5
9	1	5	7	4	2	8	3	6
4	3	6	1	5	8	9	7	2
8	7	2	6	9	3	5	1	4
3	4	7	5	6	9	2	8	1
1	6	8	2	3	7	4	5	9
2	5	9	4	8	1	3	6	7

Medium Puzzle 15

5	8	6	3	1	2	4	7	9
1	7	9	6	8	4	2	3	5
4	2	3	5	9	7	1	8	6
2	5	8	4	7	3	6	9	1
6	3	4	1	2	9	7	5	8
9	1	7	8	5	6	3	2	4
8	6	1	2	3	5	9	4	7
7	4	2	9	6	8	5	1	3
3	9	5	7	4	1	8	6	2

Medium Puzzle 16

5	1	7	6	4	3	8	9	2
3	9	2	5	7	8	4	6	1
8	4	6	1	2	9	5	7	3
4	7	8	9	1	6	3	2	5
2	3	9	7	8	5	1	4	6
1	6	5	2	3	4	9	8	7
9	5	4	3	6	7	2	1	8
6	2	3	8	9	1	7	5	4
7	8	1	4	5	2	6	3	9

Medium Puzzle 17

3	7	2	6	8	1	4	5	9
4	8	6	5	9	2	3	1	7
9	5	1	7	3	4	6	8	2
7	2	8	4	5	3	9	6	1
5	3	9	2	1	6	7	4	8
6	1	4	9	7	8	2	3	5
1	6	7	3	2	5	8	9	4
2	4	5	8	6	9	1	7	3
8	9	3	1	4	7	5	2	6

Medium Puzzle 18

5	6	2	1	3	8	7	9	4
4	1	3	6	9	7	2	8	5
9	8	7	2	4	5	3	6	1
3	2	9	4	6	1	8	5	7
6	4	8	5	7	3	9	1	2
1	7	5	8	2	9	6	4	3
7	5	6	9	1	2	4	3	8
2	9	1	3	8	4	5	7	6
8	3	4	7	5	6	1	2	9

Medium Puzzle 19

5	1	9	8	2	4	3	6	7
8	2	7	1	3	6	4	9	5
4	6	3	7	9	5	8	1	2
1	8	4	5	7	9	6	2	3
3	7	6	4	8	2	9	5	1
9	5	2	3	6	1	7	4	8
7	4	5	9	1	3	2	8	6
6	3	1	2	4	8	5	7	9
2	9	8	6	5	7	1	3	4

Medium Puzzle 20

2	3	7	6	4	5	9	8	1
5	6	9	1	8	7	2	4	3
1	4	8	3	2	9	7	6	5
3	1	5	8	9	6	4	2	7
8	7	4	5	1	2	6	3	9
6	9	2	7	3	4	1	5	8
4	8	6	9	7	3	5	1	2
7	5	1	2	6	8	3	9	4
9	2	3	4	5	1	8	7	6

Medium Puzzle 21

4	7	5	9	6	2	3	8	1
2	8	3	7	1	5	6	4	9
1	9	6	4	8	3	5	2	7
7	3	9	8	4	6	2	1	5
5	6	2	1	3	9	8	7	4
8	1	4	5	2	7	9	6	3
3	4	8	2	9	1	7	5	6
9	5	1	6	7	8	4	3	2
6	2	7	3	5	4	1	9	8

Medium Puzzle 22

6	2	5	3	8	9	4	7	1
3	7	8	4	1	6	5	2	9
1	4	9	2	5	7	8	3	6
4	1	6	7	2	3	9	8	5
5	9	2	1	6	8	3	4	7
7	8	3	5	9	4	6	1	2
8	5	7	6	4	1	2	9	3
9	6	1	8	3	2	7	5	4
2	3	4	9	7	5	1	6	8

Medium Puzzle 23

7	4	2	1	8	5	3	9	6
6	8	5	9	2	3	1	7	4
1	3	9	6	7	4	5	2	8
5	9	8	2	4	6	7	3	1
3	6	7	8	5	1	9	4	2
4	2	1	3	9	7	8	6	5
8	1	3	7	6	2	4	5	9
9	5	6	4	3	8	2	1	7
2	7	4	5	1	9	6	8	3

Medium Puzzle 24

5	1	4	6	8	9	2	7	3
6	9	2	5	3	7	8	1	4
3	7	8	2	1	4	5	6	9
2	5	3	4	7	8	6	9	1
7	4	1	9	2	6	3	8	5
8	6	9	3	5	1	4	2	7
4	8	7	1	6	5	9	3	2
9	3	6	7	4	2	1	5	8
1	2	5	8	9	3	7	4	6

Medium Puzzle 25

6	5	1	7	9	8	2	3	4
2	7	3	6	5	4	8	9	1
9	8	4	3	2	1	7	5	6
4	6	2	5	1	7	3	8	9
7	3	5	8	6	9	4	1	2
8	1	9	2	4	3	6	7	5
5	4	8	9	7	6	1	2	3
3	2	6	1	8	5	9	4	7
1	9	7	4	3	2	5	6	8

Medium Puzzle 26

1	2	7	6	5	3	8	9	4
9	5	8	7	2	4	1	6	3
3	4	6	8	1	9	2	5	7
6	1	3	4	7	5	9	8	2
5	8	4	9	3	2	6	7	1
7	9	2	1	6	8	3	4	5
8	7	9	2	4	1	5	3	6
4	3	1	5	9	6	7	2	8
2	6	5	3	8	7	4	1	9

Medium Puzzle 27

2	9	4	6	1	8	5	7	3
7	5	1	2	9	3	8	4	6
6	8	3	7	5	4	9	2	1
3	1	8	5	4	2	7	6	9
5	2	6	9	8	7	1	3	4
4	7	9	1	3	6	2	5	8
9	3	2	8	6	5	4	1	7
8	6	5	4	7	1	3	9	2
1	4	7	3	2	9	6	8	5

Medium Puzzle 28

2	5	1	3	4	9	8	6	7
9	3	6	1	8	7	5	2	4
7	4	8	6	5	2	9	3	1
4	7	3	8	1	6	2	9	5
1	8	2	4	9	5	6	7	3
6	9	5	7	2	3	1	4	8
5	2	7	9	3	8	4	1	6
3	1	9	5	6	4	7	8	2
8	6	4	2	7	1	3	5	9

Medium Puzzle 29

8	9	1	6	7	2	5	4	3
5	4	6	9	1	3	7	8	2
2	3	7	4	8	5	9	6	1
7	1	5	8	4	9	3	2	6
9	6	4	3	2	7	8	1	5
3	2	8	1	5	6	4	9	7
1	5	9	2	3	8	6	7	4
4	8	3	7	6	1	2	5	9
6	7	2	5	9	4	1	3	8

Medium Puzzle 30

5	1	9	4	8	6	3	2	7
3	4	7	5	1	2	8	6	9
2	8	6	3	7	9	1	5	4
7	9	8	1	5	4	2	3	6
4	2	5	9	6	3	7	1	8
6	3	1	7	2	8	9	4	5
1	5	3	6	9	7	4	8	2
8	7	4	2	3	5	6	9	1
9	6	2	8	4	1	5	7	3

Medium Puzzle 31

3	6	1	8	5	2	9	7	4
7	9	8	6	4	1	3	5	2
4	2	5	7	3	9	1	6	8
2	7	4	3	8	5	6	9	1
6	8	9	1	2	7	5	4	3
5	1	3	4	9	6	2	8	7
1	3	6	5	7	8	4	2	9
9	4	7	2	6	3	8	1	5
8	5	2	9	1	4	7	3	6

Medium Puzzle 32

4	2	8	1	9	6	7	5	3
6	7	3	8	2	5	4	1	9
1	5	9	4	7	3	8	6	2
3	9	5	6	8	4	1	2	7
7	8	4	2	3	1	5	9	6
2	1	6	9	5	7	3	4	8
8	3	1	5	6	2	9	7	4
9	4	2	7	1	8	6	3	5
5	6	7	3	4	9	2	8	1

Medium Puzzle 33

7	9	1	8	4	2	3	6	5
6	2	4	5	7	3	9	1	8
5	3	8	1	6	9	7	4	2
3	1	2	6	8	4	5	7	9
8	5	6	7	9	1	2	3	4
4	7	9	2	3	5	1	8	6
2	6	7	3	5	8	4	9	1
9	8	5	4	1	7	6	2	3
1	4	3	9	2	6	8	5	7

Medium Puzzle 34

5	9	7	8	3	4	1	6	2
3	8	1	6	2	9	7	4	5
2	4	6	5	1	7	8	9	3
6	5	2	9	4	8	3	7	1
8	7	4	1	5	3	9	2	6
9	1	3	7	6	2	4	5	8
4	6	9	2	8	1	5	3	7
7	2	8	3	9	5	6	1	4
1	3	5	4	7	6	2	8	9

Medium Puzzle 35

6	2	4	1	5	8	9	7	3
5	3	7	2	6	9	1	8	4
1	8	9	3	4	7	5	2	6
2	9	3	8	1	6	4	5	7
8	1	6	4	7	5	2	3	9
7	4	5	9	3	2	8	6	1
4	7	2	5	9	3	6	1	8
9	6	8	7	2	1	3	4	5
3	5	1	6	8	4	7	9	2

Medium Puzzle 36

6	8	4	1	7	5	3	2	9
9	2	3	6	4	8	5	7	1
1	7	5	9	2	3	8	6	4
8	4	1	3	6	7	2	9	5
3	6	9	5	8	2	4	1	7
2	5	7	4	1	9	6	8	3
7	1	6	2	3	4	9	5	8
5	3	8	7	9	6	1	4	2
4	9	2	8	5	1	7	3	6

Medium Puzzle 37

7	3	4	9	5	8	1	6	2
2	6	1	3	4	7	9	5	8
9	8	5	1	6	2	4	3	7
3	4	8	7	2	5	6	1	9
1	7	6	8	9	4	5	2	3
5	9	2	6	1	3	7	8	4
8	2	9	5	7	1	3	4	6
4	1	7	2	3	6	8	9	5
6	5	3	4	8	9	2	7	1

Medium Puzzle 38

8	7	3	6	4	5	2	9	1
6	5	9	1	2	3	4	8	7
4	2	1	9	8	7	5	3	6
3	1	8	5	9	6	7	2	4
2	4	5	7	3	8	6	1	9
7	9	6	2	1	4	8	5	3
5	6	2	3	7	9	1	4	8
1	3	4	8	6	2	9	7	5
9	8	7	4	5	1	3	6	2

Medium Puzzle 39

5	2	7	3	9	4	6	8	1
1	3	8	2	5	6	4	7	9
4	6	9	1	8	7	5	2	3
9	8	1	7	2	5	3	4	6
3	4	2	6	1	9	7	5	8
7	5	6	8	4	3	1	9	2
6	1	4	9	7	8	2	3	5
2	9	5	4	3	1	8	6	7
8	7	3	5	6	2	9	1	4

Medium Puzzle 40

2	7	8	6	1	5	4	9	3
9	5	6	4	3	7	2	8	1
1	4	3	8	9	2	7	5	6
6	1	5	9	8	4	3	7	2
7	8	9	2	6	3	1	4	5
3	2	4	7	5	1	9	6	8
5	9	1	3	4	6	8	2	7
4	6	2	1	7	8	5	3	9
8	3	7	5	2	9	6	1	4

Medium Puzzle 41

7	6	8	5	1	2	4	9	3
4	3	1	6	9	7	5	8	2
5	9	2	3	8	4	7	1	6
1	4	7	9	2	6	3	5	8
3	5	9	8	4	1	2	6	7
2	8	6	7	5	3	9	4	1
6	1	5	2	7	9	8	3	4
8	2	4	1	3	5	6	7	9
9	7	3	4	6	8	1	2	5

Medium Puzzle 42

6	7	4	1	5	9	8	3	2
9	1	5	3	2	8	4	6	7
8	2	3	6	7	4	9	1	5
3	5	6	8	9	1	7	2	4
7	4	9	2	6	5	1	8	3
2	8	1	4	3	7	6	5	9
5	9	2	7	1	6	3	4	8
4	6	7	5	8	3	2	9	1
1	3	8	9	4	2	5	7	6

Medium Puzzle 43

8	5	1	7	6	2	4	9	3
6	2	9	3	5	4	8	1	7
7	3	4	9	1	8	5	6	2
5	1	8	4	2	6	3	7	9
9	4	3	1	7	5	2	8	6
2	6	7	8	3	9	1	4	5
1	8	5	2	9	7	6	3	4
4	9	2	6	8	3	7	5	1
3	7	6	5	4	1	9	2	8

Medium Puzzle 44

1	7	6	3	4	2	5	9	8
3	8	5	9	1	6	7	4	2
2	4	9	5	7	8	3	6	1
5	9	2	4	6	1	8	3	7
4	1	7	8	2	3	6	5	9
8	6	3	7	5	9	1	2	4
6	3	1	2	9	7	4	8	5
9	5	8	1	3	4	2	7	6
7	2	4	6	8	5	9	1	3

Medium Puzzle 45

9	6	7	3	4	8	5	2	1
4	8	2	1	7	5	9	3	6
3	5	1	9	6	2	7	4	8
6	2	9	7	8	4	1	5	3
1	7	5	2	3	9	6	8	4
8	4	3	6	5	1	2	7	9
2	9	8	5	1	3	4	6	7
7	1	4	8	2	6	3	9	5
5	3	6	4	9	7	8	1	2

Medium Puzzle 46

4	9	7	5	6	3	8	1	2
3	2	1	9	8	7	6	5	4
5	6	8	4	1	2	7	3	9
2	4	5	8	3	9	1	7	6
9	1	3	7	2	6	4	8	5
8	7	6	1	4	5	2	9	3
1	5	2	3	7	4	9	6	8
7	3	4	6	9	8	5	2	1
6	8	9	2	5	1	3	4	7

Medium Puzzle 47

5	9	7	8	1	3	2	6	4
8	3	2	6	4	9	7	1	5
6	1	4	2	5	7	8	3	9
9	5	3	7	2	1	4	8	6
1	2	6	4	9	8	5	7	3
4	7	8	5	3	6	1	9	2
7	4	9	1	6	2	3	5	8
2	6	1	3	8	5	9	4	7
3	8	5	9	7	4	6	2	1

Medium Puzzle 48

9	8	7	1	3	6	4	2	5
4	5	1	8	2	7	3	6	9
2	6	3	5	4	9	1	8	7
6	4	9	2	1	5	8	7	3
7	1	5	9	8	3	2	4	6
3	2	8	7	6	4	9	5	1
8	9	6	4	5	1	7	3	2
1	3	2	6	7	8	5	9	4
5	7	4	3	9	2	6	1	8

Medium Puzzle 49

6	8	9	7	2	4	3	5	1
3	7	2	1	8	5	9	6	4
5	1	4	3	6	9	2	8	7
4	9	5	2	7	8	6	1	3
8	2	1	4	3	6	7	9	5
7	3	6	9	5	1	4	2	8
1	5	3	6	4	2	8	7	9
9	6	7	8	1	3	5	4	2
2	4	8	5	9	7	1	3	6

Medium Puzzle 50

4	6	5	9	1	7	8	2	3
9	3	8	2	4	5	7	1	6
2	7	1	3	8	6	4	5	9
5	8	9	7	3	4	2	6	1
3	2	4	8	6	1	9	7	5
6	1	7	5	2	9	3	4	8
8	5	6	4	9	2	1	3	7
1	4	3	6	7	8	5	9	2
7	9	2	1	5	3	6	8	4

Medium Puzzle 51

1	8	2	9	3	5	6	7	4
5	7	3	8	4	6	1	2	9
6	4	9	7	2	1	3	8	5
7	2	5	4	6	3	9	1	8
8	9	4	2	1	7	5	6	3
3	1	6	5	9	8	7	4	2
9	5	8	1	7	4	2	3	6
4	6	1	3	5	2	8	9	7
2	3	7	6	8	9	4	5	1

Medium Puzzle 52

4	8	3	6	5	7	1	2	9
5	6	1	3	2	9	7	8	4
7	9	2	4	8	1	6	3	5
3	4	7	5	6	2	9	1	8
6	2	8	9	1	3	4	5	7
1	5	9	8	7	4	2	6	3
9	7	6	1	3	8	5	4	2
2	3	5	7	4	6	8	9	1
8	1	4	2	9	5	3	7	6

Medium Puzzle 53

7	4	1	2	9	3	5	8	6
6	5	9	8	7	1	2	3	4
3	2	8	4	6	5	1	7	9
4	9	6	5	8	7	3	1	2
2	8	7	3	1	4	6	9	5
5	1	3	9	2	6	8	4	7
9	7	5	1	3	2	4	6	8
1	6	2	7	4	8	9	5	3
8	3	4	6	5	9	7	2	1

Medium Puzzle 54

4	9	8	1	2	6	3	5	7
7	3	1	4	5	9	2	8	6
6	5	2	3	7	8	4	9	1
2	6	7	5	4	3	8	1	9
1	8	9	2	6	7	5	3	4
3	4	5	9	8	1	7	6	2
5	1	6	7	3	2	9	4	8
9	7	4	8	1	5	6	2	3
8	2	3	6	9	4	1	7	5

Medium Puzzle 55

7	3	2	8	6	5	1	9	4
9	4	1	3	2	7	8	6	5
8	5	6	9	1	4	2	7	3
1	7	9	6	5	3	4	2	8
3	8	4	7	9	2	5	1	6
6	2	5	1	4	8	9	3	7
5	1	7	4	3	9	6	8	2
2	9	3	5	8	6	7	4	1
4	6	8	2	7	1	3	5	9

Medium Puzzle 56

2	7	6	4	9	3	8	1	5
1	9	3	8	2	5	7	6	4
5	8	4	7	6	1	2	9	3
6	2	8	5	1	7	4	3	9
4	1	9	6	3	8	5	2	7
3	5	7	2	4	9	1	8	6
9	4	1	3	7	2	6	5	8
7	3	5	1	8	6	9	4	2
8	6	2	9	5	4	3	7	1

Medium Puzzle 57

4	8	3	6	5	7	1	2	9
5	6	1	3	2	9	7	8	4
7	9	2	4	8	1	6	3	5
3	4	7	5	6	2	9	1	8
6	2	8	9	1	3	4	5	7
1	5	9	8	7	4	2	6	3
9	7	6	1	3	8	5	4	2
2	3	5	7	4	6	8	9	1
8	1	4	2	9	5	3	7	6

Medium Puzzle 58

8	1	3	9	2	7	5	4	6
9	4	6	1	8	5	7	2	3
2	5	7	4	3	6	9	8	1
7	2	9	5	4	1	6	3	8
1	3	4	7	6	8	2	5	9
6	8	5	2	9	3	4	1	7
5	6	1	8	7	4	3	9	2
4	7	2	3	1	9	8	6	5
3	9	8	6	5	2	1	7	4

Medium Puzzle 59

8	4	5	6	1	3	2	7	9
7	6	3	9	2	5	8	1	4
1	2	9	8	7	4	6	3	5
5	1	8	7	9	2	4	6	3
2	9	4	3	6	1	5	8	7
3	7	6	4	5	8	1	9	2
4	3	7	2	8	6	9	5	1
6	5	2	1	3	9	7	4	8
9	8	1	5	4	7	3	2	6

Medium Puzzle 60

3	1	2	9	4	6	5	8	7
6	8	5	7	2	3	1	9	4
4	7	9	1	5	8	2	6	3
1	9	8	4	6	2	7	3	5
7	4	6	3	9	5	8	2	1
5	2	3	8	1	7	6	4	9
2	5	4	6	7	9	3	1	8
9	3	7	2	8	1	4	5	6
8	6	1	5	3	4	9	7	2

Medium Puzzle 61

7	3	8	6	2	9	4	1	5
1	6	5	4	7	3	2	9	8
2	9	4	5	8	1	6	3	7
5	1	2	9	3	6	8	7	4
4	8	3	7	1	5	9	6	2
9	7	6	8	4	2	1	5	3
8	5	9	3	6	4	7	2	1
3	4	1	2	9	7	5	8	6
6	2	7	1	5	8	3	4	9

Medium Puzzle 62

3	7	5	2	1	4	8	6	9
8	6	9	3	5	7	1	4	2
2	1	4	9	8	6	3	5	7
5	4	7	6	9	3	2	8	1
6	3	8	7	2	1	4	9	5
9	2	1	8	4	5	7	3	6
1	8	6	4	7	9	5	2	3
4	5	3	1	6	2	9	7	8
7	9	2	5	3	8	6	1	4

Medium Puzzle 63

6	8	5	4	3	1	2	7	9
3	2	7	6	9	8	1	4	5
9	1	4	5	2	7	3	6	8
4	7	3	8	1	6	9	5	2
2	6	1	9	7	5	4	8	3
8	5	9	2	4	3	7	1	6
1	3	6	7	8	9	5	2	4
7	4	8	3	5	2	6	9	1
5	9	2	1	6	4	8	3	7

Medium Puzzle 64

6	2	9	4	5	8	1	3	7
3	1	8	6	7	9	2	5	4
4	5	7	2	1	3	9	8	6
7	4	3	1	6	2	8	9	5
5	8	1	9	3	4	6	7	2
9	6	2	5	8	7	4	1	3
1	3	4	7	9	6	5	2	8
2	7	5	8	4	1	3	6	9
8	9	6	3	2	5	7	4	1

Medium Puzzle 65

5	3	7	1	6	2	4	9	8
2	8	4	3	9	7	1	6	5
9	6	1	5	4	8	3	7	2
6	4	3	2	7	5	9	8	1
8	2	9	6	1	3	5	4	7
1	7	5	4	8	9	2	3	6
7	9	2	8	5	4	6	1	3
4	5	6	7	3	1	8	2	9
3	1	8	9	2	6	7	5	4

Medium Puzzle 66

9	2	7	1	6	4	8	3	5
6	3	8	5	2	7	4	9	1
5	4	1	8	3	9	2	7	6
2	1	3	6	4	5	9	8	7
7	5	4	9	8	1	6	2	3
8	9	6	2	7	3	1	5	4
4	8	9	7	5	6	3	1	2
1	6	5	3	9	2	7	4	8
3	7	2	4	1	8	5	6	9

Medium Puzzle 67

7	8	4	2	3	5	6	9	1
5	6	3	9	1	8	7	4	2
2	1	9	6	7	4	3	5	8
9	5	7	3	6	2	1	8	4
1	4	6	5	8	9	2	3	7
3	2	8	7	4	1	5	6	9
8	9	2	1	5	3	4	7	6
6	3	1	4	9	7	8	2	5
4	7	5	8	2	6	9	1	3

Medium Puzzle 68

7	6	9	4	5	8	2	1	3
2	4	1	6	7	3	5	8	9
3	8	5	9	2	1	7	4	6
1	3	8	2	4	9	6	5	7
9	7	6	3	1	5	8	2	4
4	5	2	7	8	6	3	9	1
5	9	7	1	6	2	4	3	8
8	1	4	5	3	7	9	6	2
6	2	3	8	9	4	1	7	5

Medium Puzzle 69

1	7	6	5	2	4	9	8	3
9	2	5	8	1	3	4	6	7
4	8	3	7	6	9	1	5	2
8	9	2	1	5	6	3	7	4
3	5	7	2	4	8	6	1	9
6	4	1	9	3	7	8	2	5
5	1	4	6	9	2	7	3	8
7	6	9	3	8	5	2	4	1
2	3	8	4	7	1	5	9	6

Medium Puzzle 70

7	5	8	1	3	2	6	4	9
4	1	9	7	8	6	5	3	2
3	6	2	5	4	9	7	8	1
2	3	1	8	6	4	9	5	7
5	9	6	3	7	1	4	2	8
8	7	4	9	2	5	3	1	6
9	2	7	4	5	8	1	6	3
6	4	3	2	1	7	8	9	5
1	8	5	6	9	3	2	7	4

Medium Puzzle 71

4	5	6	9	3	7	1	2	8
8	9	1	2	5	6	3	4	7
7	3	2	4	8	1	5	6	9
6	8	7	5	2	9	4	1	3
1	4	5	8	7	3	2	9	6
3	2	9	1	6	4	8	7	5
2	7	4	3	9	5	6	8	1
9	1	3	6	4	8	7	5	2
5	6	8	7	1	2	9	3	4

Medium Puzzle 72

7	4	3	2	6	5	9	1	8
1	8	6	4	9	7	5	2	3
9	2	5	3	8	1	6	4	7
8	6	9	1	3	2	4	7	5
3	7	4	6	5	9	1	8	2
2	5	1	7	4	8	3	9	6
4	3	7	8	1	6	2	5	9
6	9	2	5	7	4	8	3	1
5	1	8	9	2	3	7	6	4

Medium Puzzle 73

3	4	9	5	1	7	6	8	2
7	5	1	2	6	8	3	9	4
8	6	2	9	4	3	1	7	5
1	2	3	7	5	4	8	6	9
6	7	8	1	9	2	4	5	3
5	9	4	8	3	6	2	1	7
2	1	5	4	8	9	7	3	6
4	8	6	3	7	5	9	2	1
9	3	7	6	2	1	5	4	8

Medium Puzzle 74

9	4	1	8	2	3	6	7	5
5	3	2	1	7	6	8	9	4
7	6	8	9	4	5	2	1	3
2	1	3	6	5	9	4	8	7
4	5	7	2	3	8	9	6	1
8	9	6	7	1	4	5	3	2
1	8	5	4	6	7	3	2	9
3	7	9	5	8	2	1	4	6
6	2	4	3	9	1	7	5	8

Medium Puzzle 75

4	9	6	3	7	8	1	2	5
8	1	2	9	5	6	7	3	4
5	7	3	1	4	2	8	9	6
6	4	5	7	9	3	2	8	1
2	3	1	4	8	5	9	6	7
9	8	7	2	6	1	5	4	3
3	2	8	5	1	4	6	7	9
7	5	4	6	2	9	3	1	8
1	6	9	8	3	7	4	5	2

Medium Puzzle 76

8	7	1	2	6	3	5	4	9
3	2	5	1	9	4	8	6	7
4	6	9	8	7	5	2	3	1
7	5	4	3	2	9	1	8	6
6	8	3	4	1	7	9	2	5
9	1	2	6	5	8	4	7	3
1	4	7	5	8	6	3	9	2
2	3	6	9	4	1	7	5	8
5	9	8	7	3	2	6	1	4

Medium Puzzle 77

1	5	7	3	6	8	9	2	4
4	3	2	5	1	9	6	8	7
9	8	6	4	2	7	5	3	1
7	6	5	8	4	2	1	9	3
2	1	8	9	3	6	7	4	5
3	9	4	1	7	5	2	6	8
5	7	3	6	9	4	8	1	2
8	4	9	2	5	1	3	7	6
6	2	1	7	8	3	4	5	9

Medium Puzzle 78

5	9	1	4	3	8	7	2	6
2	7	6	9	1	5	3	4	8
8	3	4	2	7	6	1	5	9
6	5	7	8	2	4	9	1	3
3	1	2	7	6	9	4	8	5
4	8	9	1	5	3	2	6	7
1	2	8	5	9	7	6	3	4
9	6	5	3	4	2	8	7	1
7	4	3	6	8	1	5	9	2

Medium Puzzle 79

6	2	8	7	5	4	3	9	1
3	4	7	9	8	1	5	6	2
1	9	5	3	6	2	7	4	8
5	6	9	4	1	8	2	7	3
8	7	2	6	3	5	4	1	9
4	3	1	2	7	9	6	8	5
2	8	6	1	4	3	9	5	7
9	1	4	5	2	7	8	3	6
7	5	3	8	9	6	1	2	4

Medium Puzzle 80

4	9	1	3	7	5	2	6	8
5	6	8	4	1	2	7	3	9
7	2	3	9	6	8	5	4	1
2	4	5	6	3	1	8	9	7
8	7	9	5	2	4	6	1	3
1	3	6	8	9	7	4	5	2
3	8	7	1	5	6	9	2	4
6	1	4	2	8	9	3	7	5
9	5	2	7	4	3	1	8	6

Medium Puzzle 81

9	7	8	2	4	1	6	3	5
1	3	5	9	8	6	4	2	7
6	2	4	5	7	3	1	8	9
2	6	1	8	5	7	9	4	3
5	8	3	1	9	4	2	7	6
7	4	9	6	3	2	8	5	1
3	9	6	7	2	8	5	1	4
4	1	2	3	6	5	7	9	8
8	5	7	4	1	9	3	6	2

Medium Puzzle 82

7	3	9	8	1	2	5	6	4
4	1	8	7	5	6	9	2	3
6	2	5	9	3	4	7	1	8
5	8	3	6	4	1	2	9	7
9	6	7	3	2	8	4	5	1
1	4	2	5	7	9	3	8	6
2	7	6	1	9	3	8	4	5
3	9	1	4	8	5	6	7	2
8	5	4	2	6	7	1	3	9

Medium Puzzle 83

1	8	9	4	6	7	2	3	5
6	3	5	2	1	9	4	7	8
7	4	2	8	3	5	1	9	6
4	2	7	1	9	8	5	6	3
5	9	3	6	7	4	8	1	2
8	1	6	5	2	3	7	4	9
9	5	4	7	8	6	3	2	1
2	6	8	3	4	1	9	5	7
3	7	1	9	5	2	6	8	4

Medium Puzzle 84

3	4	1	5	6	2	7	9	8
8	6	9	1	3	7	2	5	4
5	2	7	4	9	8	1	6	3
1	9	3	8	7	4	5	2	6
2	5	8	6	1	3	9	4	7
4	7	6	2	5	9	8	3	1
7	1	2	3	4	5	6	8	9
9	3	5	7	8	6	4	1	2
6	8	4	9	2	1	3	7	5

Medium Puzzle 85

9	8	6	4	1	7	3	2	5
2	3	1	9	8	5	4	6	7
7	4	5	3	2	6	8	9	1
6	7	8	1	4	3	9	5	2
3	5	2	8	7	9	1	4	6
4	1	9	5	6	2	7	8	3
5	9	7	2	3	4	6	1	8
1	2	3	6	9	8	5	7	4
8	6	4	7	5	1	2	3	9

Medium Puzzle 86

6	7	4	8	2	1	3	5	9
9	1	3	7	4	5	6	8	2
8	2	5	9	3	6	1	7	4
4	8	6	3	9	2	7	1	5
2	5	1	6	7	8	4	9	3
3	9	7	5	1	4	2	6	8
1	6	2	4	8	9	5	3	7
5	3	9	2	6	7	8	4	1
7	4	8	1	5	3	9	2	6

Medium Puzzle 87

4	1	7	5	6	3	2	9	8
3	2	6	8	1	9	5	7	4
9	5	8	2	4	7	1	3	6
5	4	1	7	8	2	3	6	9
2	7	3	1	9	6	4	8	5
6	8	9	4	3	5	7	2	1
7	6	4	9	2	1	8	5	3
1	3	2	6	5	8	9	4	7
8	9	5	3	7	4	6	1	2

Medium Puzzle 88

7	1	3	8	2	4	5	9	6
6	2	9	3	1	5	4	8	7
8	4	5	7	9	6	1	3	2
5	3	4	9	6	1	2	7	8
1	9	7	5	8	2	6	4	3
2	8	6	4	3	7	9	1	5
3	5	1	6	4	8	7	2	9
4	6	8	2	7	9	3	5	1
9	7	2	1	5	3	8	6	4

Medium Puzzle 89

1	2	5	8	4	6	7	9	3
6	9	7	5	3	2	4	1	8
8	4	3	1	7	9	6	5	2
2	8	1	4	6	7	5	3	9
5	7	9	3	8	1	2	4	6
4	3	6	2	9	5	1	8	7
9	6	4	7	5	8	3	2	1
3	1	8	6	2	4	9	7	5
7	5	2	9	1	3	8	6	4

Medium Puzzle 90

8	2	5	1	3	7	4	9	6
1	6	4	5	9	2	3	7	8
3	9	7	4	8	6	1	5	2
2	1	8	3	7	5	9	6	4
4	3	9	6	2	1	5	8	7
7	5	6	9	4	8	2	1	3
5	7	1	2	6	4	8	3	9
6	4	3	8	1	9	7	2	5
9	8	2	7	5	3	6	4	1

Medium Puzzle 91

3	1	8	7	9	4	2	5	6
7	9	6	1	5	2	8	4	3
5	2	4	3	6	8	1	7	9
4	6	2	5	1	9	7	3	8
8	5	9	4	7	3	6	1	2
1	7	3	8	2	6	5	9	4
9	8	5	2	4	7	3	6	1
2	4	7	6	3	1	9	8	5
6	3	1	9	8	5	4	2	7

Medium Puzzle 92

1	7	4	5	2	9	6	8	3
3	8	6	1	7	4	5	9	2
2	5	9	3	6	8	7	1	4
8	4	3	2	5	7	9	6	1
6	2	1	8	9	3	4	5	7
5	9	7	6	4	1	2	3	8
4	1	2	9	3	5	8	7	6
7	3	5	4	8	6	1	2	9
9	6	8	7	1	2	3	4	5

Medium Puzzle 93

1	9	8	7	3	5	6	4	2
6	7	4	2	8	9	1	5	3
2	3	5	1	4	6	7	9	8
8	1	6	9	7	4	2	3	5
9	4	3	6	5	2	8	1	7
7	5	2	3	1	8	9	6	4
4	2	1	8	6	3	5	7	9
3	6	9	5	2	7	4	8	1
5	8	7	4	9	1	3	2	6

Medium Puzzle 94

8	6	4	1	7	5	3	9	2
2	5	9	4	6	3	8	1	7
1	7	3	9	2	8	5	4	6
7	4	2	5	1	9	6	3	8
3	9	8	2	4	6	7	5	1
6	1	5	3	8	7	9	2	4
4	3	6	7	5	2	1	8	9
9	2	7	8	3	1	4	6	5
5	8	1	6	9	4	2	7	3

Medium Puzzle 95

2	8	4	5	1	3	7	9	6
1	5	3	7	6	9	4	8	2
7	6	9	4	2	8	5	3	1
9	4	5	3	7	6	2	1	8
8	7	1	2	9	4	6	5	3
3	2	6	1	8	5	9	7	4
4	1	8	9	5	2	3	6	7
6	9	2	8	3	7	1	4	5
5	3	7	6	4	1	8	2	9

Medium Puzzle 96

2	5	9	4	6	8	1	3	7
8	3	6	1	7	2	5	9	4
1	4	7	3	9	5	2	6	8
6	8	3	9	2	1	7	4	5
4	7	2	5	8	3	9	1	6
5	9	1	6	4	7	3	8	2
3	2	4	7	1	6	8	5	9
9	1	8	2	5	4	6	7	3
7	6	5	8	3	9	4	2	1

Medium Puzzle 97

1	3	2	6	7	9	4	5	8
4	9	8	1	3	5	7	6	2
6	5	7	4	8	2	9	3	1
5	8	4	9	6	1	3	2	7
9	6	3	7	2	4	1	8	5
2	7	1	3	5	8	6	4	9
8	4	9	5	1	3	2	7	6
3	2	6	8	9	7	5	1	4
7	1	5	2	4	6	8	9	3

Medium Puzzle 98

4	5	7	2	6	9	3	1	8
2	6	9	8	3	1	7	4	5
8	1	3	5	4	7	6	9	2
7	3	8	9	1	5	4	2	6
6	2	1	4	8	3	9	5	7
5	9	4	6	7	2	1	8	3
9	7	5	3	2	4	8	6	1
1	4	6	7	5	8	2	3	9
3	8	2	1	9	6	5	7	4

Medium Puzzle 99

5	7	2	6	3	4	9	8	1
4	8	3	1	7	9	5	6	2
6	9	1	5	2	8	7	4	3
8	2	5	4	1	3	6	9	7
9	3	4	7	6	2	8	1	5
1	6	7	9	8	5	2	3	4
7	4	9	8	5	1	3	2	6
3	1	6	2	9	7	4	5	8
2	5	8	3	4	6	1	7	9

Medium Puzzle 100

5	6	8	3	9	1	7	4	2
9	1	2	4	7	6	3	8	5
3	7	4	8	5	2	9	6	1
6	3	5	1	4	9	8	2	7
2	8	1	5	6	7	4	9	3
4	9	7	2	8	3	5	1	6
1	5	3	9	2	4	6	7	8
7	2	9	6	3	8	1	5	4
8	4	6	7	1	5	2	3	9

Medium Puzzle 101

7	3	6	9	8	2	1	5	4
8	4	1	3	7	5	6	2	9
5	9	2	1	4	6	7	3	8
6	7	9	5	3	8	4	1	2
2	8	3	4	6	1	5	9	7
1	5	4	7	2	9	3	8	6
9	1	8	6	5	4	2	7	3
3	6	5	2	9	7	8	4	1
4	2	7	8	1	3	9	6	5

Medium Puzzle 102

2	9	3	8	7	6	4	5	1
7	5	4	3	9	1	6	2	8
6	1	8	4	5	2	9	3	7
3	2	9	6	1	8	7	4	5
5	4	1	9	3	7	8	6	2
8	7	6	5	2	4	3	1	9
4	8	2	1	6	9	5	7	3
9	3	7	2	4	5	1	8	6
1	6	5	7	8	3	2	9	4

Medium Puzzle 103

1	6	8	3	7	9	5	4	2
5	4	3	6	1	2	9	8	7
2	7	9	4	8	5	3	1	6
6	2	4	7	3	8	1	5	9
7	9	1	5	6	4	8	2	3
3	8	5	9	2	1	7	6	4
8	3	7	1	4	6	2	9	5
9	1	6	2	5	3	4	7	8
4	5	2	8	9	7	6	3	1

Medium Puzzle 104

5	2	3	6	4	8	7	1	9
8	1	6	2	7	9	5	4	3
7	9	4	5	1	3	6	8	2
6	5	7	4	8	2	3	9	1
9	8	1	3	5	7	4	2	6
4	3	2	1	9	6	8	7	5
1	4	8	9	6	5	2	3	7
3	7	5	8	2	1	9	6	4
2	6	9	7	3	4	1	5	8

Medium Puzzle 105

7	1	5	2	8	6	3	9	4
4	2	6	9	3	7	1	8	5
9	8	3	1	4	5	7	2	6
1	9	4	7	2	8	5	6	3
8	5	2	6	1	3	9	4	7
6	3	7	5	9	4	8	1	2
3	4	9	8	5	2	6	7	1
5	7	1	4	6	9	2	3	8
2	6	8	3	7	1	4	5	9

Medium Puzzle 106

1	8	4	6	9	2	5	3	7
5	9	6	7	3	1	4	2	8
3	2	7	4	8	5	1	6	9
7	1	3	5	4	8	6	9	2
6	4	2	3	1	9	8	7	5
8	5	9	2	6	7	3	4	1
4	7	1	9	5	3	2	8	6
2	3	8	1	7	6	9	5	4
9	6	5	8	2	4	7	1	3

Medium Puzzle 107

8	5	1	7	2	9	3	4	6
9	3	2	8	4	6	1	5	7
7	6	4	5	1	3	2	8	9
6	4	3	9	7	8	5	2	1
5	8	7	2	6	1	9	3	4
1	2	9	4	3	5	6	7	8
3	9	8	1	5	7	4	6	2
4	1	6	3	8	2	7	9	5
2	7	5	6	9	4	8	1	3

Medium Puzzle 108

9	5	1	2	4	7	8	6	3
4	8	7	6	3	1	2	5	9
6	2	3	5	9	8	4	7	1
8	1	6	3	7	4	9	2	5
5	7	4	9	1	2	6	3	8
3	9	2	8	6	5	1	4	7
2	6	8	7	5	9	3	1	4
1	3	5	4	8	6	7	9	2
7	4	9	1	2	3	5	8	6

Medium Puzzle 109

9	3	6	4	5	1	2	8	7
4	1	5	2	7	8	9	3	6
8	7	2	6	3	9	5	1	4
3	9	7	8	4	6	1	5	2
2	8	4	5	1	3	6	7	9
6	5	1	7	9	2	3	4	8
5	4	9	3	6	7	8	2	1
7	6	8	1	2	5	4	9	3
1	2	3	9	8	4	7	6	5

Medium Puzzle 110

1	8	3	6	4	9	2	5	7
2	6	4	5	7	8	1	3	9
5	9	7	2	1	3	6	8	4
3	1	5	7	6	2	4	9	8
8	4	6	3	9	1	7	2	5
9	7	2	4	8	5	3	1	6
6	3	9	8	2	4	5	7	1
7	2	8	1	5	6	9	4	3
4	5	1	9	3	7	8	6	2

Medium Puzzle 111

5	6	4	8	3	9	1	2	7
8	2	9	6	7	1	4	5	3
1	7	3	2	4	5	8	6	9
2	9	6	4	1	8	3	7	5
3	1	7	5	9	2	6	4	8
4	8	5	7	6	3	2	9	1
7	3	2	1	5	4	9	8	6
6	4	1	9	8	7	5	3	2
9	5	8	3	2	6	7	1	4

Medium Puzzle 112

2	8	7	5	6	1	3	9	4
4	3	5	2	9	8	7	6	1
9	6	1	7	4	3	5	2	8
6	5	3	9	1	2	8	4	7
1	2	8	3	7	4	9	5	6
7	9	4	6	8	5	1	3	2
5	1	2	8	3	6	4	7	9
8	7	6	4	5	9	2	1	3
3	4	9	1	2	7	6	8	5

Medium Puzzle 113

2	3	9	6	7	1	8	4	5
5	8	7	9	4	2	1	6	3
6	1	4	8	3	5	7	9	2
1	5	8	2	9	6	3	7	4
3	4	6	7	5	8	2	1	9
9	7	2	4	1	3	5	8	6
7	6	5	3	8	9	4	2	1
8	2	3	1	6	4	9	5	7
4	9	1	5	2	7	6	3	8

Medium Puzzle 114

7	1	5	4	6	2	3	8	9
9	3	4	5	1	8	6	7	2
6	8	2	7	3	9	4	1	5
2	5	7	8	9	3	1	4	6
8	4	1	6	2	7	9	5	3
3	6	9	1	5	4	8	2	7
4	7	3	9	8	5	2	6	1
5	9	6	2	4	1	7	3	8
1	2	8	3	7	6	5	9	4

Medium Puzzle 115

8	7	4	3	5	1	6	9	2
5	6	2	7	9	4	1	8	3
9	1	3	6	8	2	4	5	7
2	9	5	1	7	6	8	3	4
4	8	6	2	3	9	5	7	1
1	3	7	5	4	8	9	2	6
7	5	1	8	6	3	2	4	9
6	4	8	9	2	7	3	1	5
3	2	9	4	1	5	7	6	8

Medium Puzzle 116

3	5	4	2	1	9	6	8	7
9	2	7	4	8	6	5	1	3
8	1	6	3	7	5	2	9	4
7	9	5	8	6	1	3	4	2
2	8	3	9	4	7	1	5	6
4	6	1	5	2	3	8	7	9
1	4	2	7	3	8	9	6	5
6	7	9	1	5	2	4	3	8
5	3	8	6	9	4	7	2	1

Medium Puzzle 117

2	8	3	1	6	4	7	5	9
6	9	4	5	7	3	1	2	8
7	1	5	9	8	2	3	6	4
8	4	6	7	3	9	2	1	5
3	5	7	2	1	8	4	9	6
9	2	1	6	4	5	8	3	7
5	7	8	3	9	1	6	4	2
1	6	2	4	5	7	9	8	3
4	3	9	8	2	6	5	7	1

Medium Puzzle 118

4	3	5	8	2	7	9	6	1
6	2	8	9	4	1	5	3	7
1	9	7	5	6	3	8	4	2
7	6	9	2	3	8	4	1	5
8	1	3	4	5	6	7	2	9
5	4	2	1	7	9	3	8	6
3	8	1	7	9	2	6	5	4
9	5	6	3	1	4	2	7	8
2	7	4	6	8	5	1	9	3

Medium Puzzle 119

9	4	1	7	2	8	5	6	3
5	8	7	3	6	1	4	9	2
2	3	6	5	4	9	1	7	8
6	2	3	4	9	5	8	1	7
7	5	4	1	8	6	2	3	9
1	9	8	2	7	3	6	4	5
8	1	2	9	3	4	7	5	6
4	7	9	6	5	2	3	8	1
3	6	5	8	1	7	9	2	4

Medium Puzzle 120

5	1	4	7	8	9	6	2	3
3	6	8	1	4	2	9	7	5
7	9	2	3	6	5	4	1	8
1	4	5	2	3	6	8	9	7
9	2	6	8	1	7	3	5	4
8	7	3	5	9	4	1	6	2
4	3	7	9	2	1	5	8	6
2	8	9	6	5	3	7	4	1
6	5	1	4	7	8	2	3	9

Medium Puzzle 121

5	3	2	8	9	4	6	7	1
8	7	1	3	5	6	9	4	2
6	4	9	2	1	7	3	5	8
7	9	4	1	3	5	8	2	6
3	6	8	7	4	2	5	1	9
2	1	5	9	6	8	4	3	7
4	8	6	5	2	1	7	9	3
9	2	7	4	8	3	1	6	5
1	5	3	6	7	9	2	8	4

Medium Puzzle 122

4	2	7	3	5	9	6	8	1
8	3	1	4	6	2	5	9	7
5	9	6	1	7	8	2	3	4
2	8	5	6	1	7	3	4	9
6	1	3	9	2	4	7	5	8
7	4	9	5	8	3	1	6	2
9	5	2	7	4	6	8	1	3
1	7	4	8	3	5	9	2	6
3	6	8	2	9	1	4	7	5

Medium Puzzle 123

8	5	1	3	2	7	6	9	4
9	6	7	5	1	4	8	3	2
2	4	3	6	9	8	5	1	7
3	2	5	4	8	9	1	7	6
7	9	6	2	5	1	3	4	8
1	8	4	7	6	3	9	2	5
4	1	2	8	3	5	7	6	9
5	7	9	1	4	6	2	8	3
6	3	8	9	7	2	4	5	1

Medium Puzzle 124

4	7	1	9	5	2	3	8	6
2	9	8	3	6	7	1	4	5
3	6	5	1	8	4	7	9	2
5	3	7	4	9	8	6	2	1
6	8	9	2	1	5	4	3	7
1	4	2	7	3	6	9	5	8
8	5	4	6	7	3	2	1	9
9	2	6	8	4	1	5	7	3
7	1	3	5	2	9	8	6	4

Medium Puzzle 125

6	1	5	7	3	9	2	4	8
7	8	3	2	6	4	5	1	9
9	2	4	8	1	5	6	3	7
4	6	9	3	5	1	7	8	2
3	5	8	4	7	2	1	9	6
1	7	2	9	8	6	3	5	4
2	4	1	6	9	3	8	7	5
5	9	7	1	2	8	4	6	3
8	3	6	5	4	7	9	2	1

Medium Puzzle 126

5	4	9	7	2	1	6	3	8
3	6	1	5	9	8	4	2	7
7	2	8	6	3	4	5	1	9
9	8	3	4	5	2	7	6	1
4	1	6	9	7	3	2	8	5
2	5	7	1	8	6	3	9	4
8	9	4	3	6	7	1	5	2
6	7	2	8	1	5	9	4	3
1	3	5	2	4	9	8	7	6

Medium Puzzle 127

2	8	1	7	6	5	9	4	3
3	9	4	8	1	2	5	7	6
7	5	6	9	4	3	2	1	8
4	1	7	5	2	8	6	3	9
8	2	9	1	3	6	4	5	7
5	6	3	4	9	7	1	8	2
1	7	2	6	8	4	3	9	5
6	4	8	3	5	9	7	2	1
9	3	5	2	7	1	8	6	4

Medium Puzzle 128

9	7	4	5	6	8	3	1	2
5	8	6	1	2	3	9	7	4
1	3	2	7	4	9	8	5	6
2	5	8	6	1	7	4	3	9
4	6	9	2	3	5	7	8	1
3	1	7	9	8	4	2	6	5
6	2	3	8	9	1	5	4	7
7	4	1	3	5	2	6	9	8
8	9	5	4	7	6	1	2	3

Medium Puzzle 129

5	4	9	7	2	6	3	1	8
6	8	3	1	5	9	7	4	2
7	2	1	4	8	3	6	9	5
3	6	4	9	1	5	8	2	7
2	7	5	6	4	8	9	3	1
1	9	8	3	7	2	4	5	6
4	5	6	8	9	1	2	7	3
9	3	2	5	6	7	1	8	4
8	1	7	2	3	4	5	6	9

Medium Puzzle 130

7	3	2	5	6	4	1	8	9
6	1	4	8	3	9	2	5	7
5	9	8	2	7	1	3	4	6
2	8	6	3	9	7	4	1	5
1	5	9	4	8	2	7	6	3
4	7	3	6	1	5	9	2	8
9	2	5	7	4	6	8	3	1
3	4	7	1	5	8	6	9	2
8	6	1	9	2	3	5	7	4

Medium Puzzle 131

6	2	3	9	1	8	4	5	7
4	9	8	6	5	7	3	2	1
5	1	7	3	4	2	6	8	9
8	5	1	7	2	6	9	3	4
7	3	4	8	9	5	1	6	2
9	6	2	4	3	1	5	7	8
2	4	5	1	7	3	8	9	6
3	8	9	2	6	4	7	1	5
1	7	6	5	8	9	2	4	3

Medium Puzzle 132

1	5	9	3	4	6	8	2	7
2	3	6	9	7	8	5	4	1
4	8	7	5	1	2	6	9	3
8	1	2	4	3	9	7	5	6
6	9	5	7	2	1	3	8	4
3	7	4	6	8	5	2	1	9
5	4	8	1	6	7	9	3	2
9	6	3	2	5	4	1	7	8
7	2	1	8	9	3	4	6	5

Medium Puzzle 133

1	2	5	7	6	3	9	4	8
7	3	8	9	5	4	2	1	6
9	6	4	8	2	1	7	3	5
2	4	1	3	7	6	5	8	9
8	7	3	5	1	9	6	2	4
6	5	9	2	4	8	3	7	1
4	9	6	1	3	2	8	5	7
3	1	7	6	8	5	4	9	2
5	8	2	4	9	7	1	6	3

Medium Puzzle 134

1	9	6	4	8	2	5	3	7
5	4	7	1	3	9	8	2	6
3	8	2	5	6	7	4	9	1
8	6	1	3	7	4	2	5	9
7	5	4	9	2	6	3	1	8
9	2	3	8	1	5	6	7	4
4	3	8	7	5	1	9	6	2
6	7	9	2	4	3	1	8	5
2	1	5	6	9	8	7	4	3

Medium Puzzle 135

5	2	9	7	1	6	4	8	3
7	6	4	3	8	9	2	1	5
3	8	1	5	2	4	7	6	9
8	7	5	4	6	2	3	9	1
1	4	6	9	3	5	8	7	2
9	3	2	1	7	8	6	5	4
6	9	3	8	4	1	5	2	7
2	1	7	6	5	3	9	4	8
4	5	8	2	9	7	1	3	6

Medium Puzzle 136

9	5	3	7	8	4	1	2	6
2	1	6	5	3	9	4	7	8
7	8	4	2	6	1	9	3	5
1	6	7	8	2	3	5	4	9
4	2	5	9	7	6	8	1	3
3	9	8	4	1	5	7	6	2
8	7	1	3	5	2	6	9	4
5	3	9	6	4	7	2	8	1
6	4	2	1	9	8	3	5	7

Medium Puzzle 137

6	1	8	2	9	3	4	5	7
5	4	3	8	1	7	6	2	9
2	7	9	5	6	4	8	1	3
8	6	4	1	7	2	9	3	5
7	3	5	9	4	8	1	6	2
1	9	2	6	3	5	7	4	8
9	2	1	3	8	6	5	7	4
4	5	6	7	2	9	3	8	1
3	8	7	4	5	1	2	9	6

Medium Puzzle 138

3	2	8	9	5	4	6	7	1
9	7	6	1	3	8	2	5	4
1	5	4	6	7	2	8	9	3
2	9	3	4	8	1	5	6	7
4	8	1	7	6	5	3	2	9
7	6	5	3	2	9	4	1	8
5	3	2	8	9	7	1	4	6
8	4	7	5	1	6	9	3	2
6	1	9	2	4	3	7	8	5

Medium Puzzle 139

9	3	1	2	4	8	5	7	6
6	5	8	9	3	7	1	2	4
2	7	4	5	1	6	8	9	3
1	2	3	4	6	5	9	8	7
5	8	7	3	9	1	6	4	2
4	9	6	7	8	2	3	1	5
3	6	9	8	7	4	2	5	1
8	4	5	1	2	3	7	6	9
7	1	2	6	5	9	4	3	8

Medium Puzzle 140

6	8	5	2	4	9	7	1	3
4	2	9	3	7	1	8	5	6
7	3	1	6	5	8	4	2	9
2	4	3	9	6	7	1	8	5
5	9	6	8	1	2	3	7	4
8	1	7	5	3	4	6	9	2
3	7	2	1	9	6	5	4	8
1	6	8	4	2	5	9	3	7
9	5	4	7	8	3	2	6	1

Medium Puzzle 141

1	3	5	2	7	9	4	6	8
7	8	6	3	1	4	5	2	9
4	2	9	6	5	8	7	3	1
6	5	1	4	3	2	9	8	7
2	7	8	1	9	6	3	5	4
9	4	3	7	8	5	6	1	2
8	9	4	5	6	1	2	7	3
3	6	2	8	4	7	1	9	5
5	1	7	9	2	3	8	4	6

Medium Puzzle 142

7	8	4	1	6	5	3	9	2
1	5	2	3	9	8	7	4	6
6	9	3	2	4	7	5	8	1
4	1	6	7	3	9	2	5	8
9	7	5	8	2	4	6	1	3
3	2	8	6	5	1	4	7	9
5	3	9	4	8	6	1	2	7
8	6	1	5	7	2	9	3	4
2	4	7	9	1	3	8	6	5

Medium Puzzle 143

4	1	6	5	7	3	9	8	2
2	8	3	4	9	1	5	7	6
5	9	7	2	8	6	4	1	3
8	5	9	6	3	7	2	4	1
1	6	4	9	5	2	8	3	7
3	7	2	1	4	8	6	9	5
9	2	1	7	6	4	3	5	8
7	3	5	8	2	9	1	6	4
6	4	8	3	1	5	7	2	9

Medium Puzzle 144

1	7	8	3	6	2	5	9	4
9	3	4	7	1	5	6	8	2
2	5	6	8	9	4	1	7	3
8	2	3	5	4	1	9	6	7
5	9	1	6	2	7	4	3	8
4	6	7	9	3	8	2	1	5
3	8	2	1	5	6	7	4	9
6	4	9	2	7	3	8	5	1
7	1	5	4	8	9	3	2	6

Medium Puzzle 145

3	1	2	4	7	5	9	8	6
7	9	4	6	1	8	2	5	3
6	8	5	3	2	9	4	1	7
4	3	8	1	9	6	5	7	2
2	6	7	8	5	4	1	3	9
1	5	9	2	3	7	8	6	4
9	7	1	5	6	2	3	4	8
8	2	3	7	4	1	6	9	5
5	4	6	9	8	3	7	2	1

Medium Puzzle 146

9	4	2	6	5	8	3	7	1
1	5	3	2	7	9	4	6	8
6	7	8	1	3	4	2	9	5
4	2	1	3	6	5	7	8	9
7	6	9	4	8	1	5	2	3
3	8	5	9	2	7	6	1	4
2	9	4	5	1	6	8	3	7
5	3	7	8	9	2	1	4	6
8	1	6	7	4	3	9	5	2

Medium Puzzle 147

9	5	3	7	1	2	8	4	6
6	4	7	3	5	8	1	2	9
2	1	8	6	4	9	5	3	7
8	7	2	9	6	4	3	1	5
3	6	4	1	2	5	9	7	8
5	9	1	8	3	7	4	6	2
1	8	5	2	7	3	6	9	4
4	2	6	5	9	1	7	8	3
7	3	9	4	8	6	2	5	1

Medium Puzzle 148

4	2	1	6	7	8	3	9	5
3	6	7	9	2	5	8	1	4
9	8	5	4	1	3	6	2	7
6	7	4	3	9	1	5	8	2
2	3	8	7	5	4	9	6	1
1	5	9	8	6	2	4	7	3
5	9	6	1	4	7	2	3	8
7	4	3	2	8	6	1	5	9
8	1	2	5	3	9	7	4	6

Medium Puzzle 149

8	4	6	3	1	5	7	9	2
1	3	7	6	2	9	5	8	4
5	9	2	8	4	7	1	3	6
3	1	9	4	7	2	8	6	5
7	5	4	9	8	6	2	1	3
6	2	8	5	3	1	9	4	7
4	6	5	7	9	8	3	2	1
9	7	1	2	6	3	4	5	8
2	8	3	1	5	4	6	7	9

Medium Puzzle 150

6	5	4	8	3	2	1	9	7
1	8	9	5	7	4	6	3	2
7	3	2	9	6	1	5	4	8
5	6	7	3	4	8	9	2	1
2	4	8	7	1	9	3	5	6
9	1	3	6	2	5	7	8	4
4	9	6	2	5	7	8	1	3
3	2	5	1	8	6	4	7	9
8	7	1	4	9	3	2	6	5

Medium Puzzle 151

6	3	2	9	8	4	5	1	7
8	1	4	5	7	2	3	6	9
5	9	7	6	3	1	4	8	2
7	6	5	3	1	8	2	9	4
4	2	3	7	6	9	1	5	8
9	8	1	4	2	5	6	7	3
3	5	9	8	4	6	7	2	1
2	7	6	1	9	3	8	4	5
1	4	8	2	5	7	9	3	6

Medium Puzzle 152

1	9	4	3	5	6	8	7	2
5	8	3	2	4	7	9	1	6
2	7	6	9	1	8	4	3	5
4	1	2	8	7	5	6	9	3
7	3	5	6	2	9	1	4	8
9	6	8	1	3	4	5	2	7
3	4	7	5	8	1	2	6	9
8	2	9	4	6	3	7	5	1
6	5	1	7	9	2	3	8	4

Medium Puzzle 153

6	8	9	3	1	4	2	7	5
2	4	7	8	6	5	9	1	3
3	5	1	2	9	7	4	8	6
8	9	3	4	7	6	1	5	2
5	7	6	1	2	3	8	9	4
1	2	4	9	5	8	3	6	7
7	1	2	5	3	9	6	4	8
4	3	5	6	8	1	7	2	9
9	6	8	7	4	2	5	3	1

Medium Puzzle 154

9	2	4	1	5	8	3	7	6
8	6	5	3	7	4	9	2	1
7	3	1	6	2	9	5	8	4
4	9	8	7	6	3	1	5	2
6	5	7	8	1	2	4	3	9
2	1	3	4	9	5	7	6	8
3	8	2	5	4	1	6	9	7
1	7	9	2	3	6	8	4	5
5	4	6	9	8	7	2	1	3

Medium Puzzle 155

6	8	3	9	7	2	1	5	4
7	2	9	5	1	4	8	3	6
1	5	4	6	3	8	2	7	9
8	3	6	4	2	7	9	1	5
2	9	1	8	5	6	7	4	3
4	7	5	1	9	3	6	8	2
3	1	7	2	4	9	5	6	8
5	6	2	3	8	1	4	9	7
9	4	8	7	6	5	3	2	1

Medium Puzzle 156

3	6	1	7	4	9	5	8	2
2	4	5	6	1	8	7	3	9
7	9	8	5	3	2	4	1	6
1	5	3	9	8	6	2	7	4
4	8	6	1	2	7	9	5	3
9	2	7	3	5	4	8	6	1
6	1	4	2	7	5	3	9	8
8	7	9	4	6	3	1	2	5
5	3	2	8	9	1	6	4	7

Medium Puzzle 157

4	2	8	9	5	3	1	6	7
1	9	3	8	6	7	4	5	2
7	6	5	2	4	1	8	3	9
9	8	4	6	7	2	3	1	5
2	7	1	5	3	8	6	9	4
5	3	6	4	1	9	2	7	8
8	1	7	3	9	4	5	2	6
6	4	9	1	2	5	7	8	3
3	5	2	7	8	6	9	4	1

Medium Puzzle 158

6	4	7	8	2	9	1	3	5
2	3	5	6	7	1	9	4	8
8	1	9	4	3	5	6	2	7
3	2	1	7	5	8	4	6	9
4	5	8	9	6	3	2	7	1
9	7	6	2	1	4	8	5	3
1	6	4	3	8	7	5	9	2
5	9	3	1	4	2	7	8	6
7	8	2	5	9	6	3	1	4

Medium Puzzle 159

1	9	3	7	2	4	6	8	5
6	2	8	5	1	3	9	7	4
5	4	7	8	6	9	2	1	3
3	8	5	6	4	7	1	9	2
4	7	6	2	9	1	5	3	8
2	1	9	3	5	8	7	4	6
9	6	1	4	3	2	8	5	7
7	5	4	9	8	6	3	2	1
8	3	2	1	7	5	4	6	9

Medium Puzzle 160

3	8	1	7	9	2	5	6	4
4	6	2	3	5	8	9	7	1
5	9	7	6	1	4	3	2	8
1	3	9	8	2	6	7	4	5
6	5	4	9	7	1	8	3	2
2	7	8	4	3	5	1	9	6
8	1	3	2	4	7	6	5	9
9	2	5	1	6	3	4	8	7
7	4	6	5	8	9	2	1	3

Medium Puzzle 161

8	5	4	1	2	3	9	7	6
6	7	2	4	8	9	3	5	1
1	9	3	6	5	7	8	4	2
5	2	8	7	4	1	6	9	3
3	1	9	2	6	5	4	8	7
7	4	6	9	3	8	1	2	5
4	8	7	5	1	6	2	3	9
2	6	5	3	9	4	7	1	8
9	3	1	8	7	2	5	6	4

Medium Puzzle 162

8	4	7	2	3	6	9	1	5
2	3	5	7	1	9	4	8	6
6	1	9	4	8	5	7	2	3
1	2	4	3	5	7	8	6	9
5	9	3	1	6	8	2	7	4
7	8	6	9	2	4	5	3	1
9	6	8	5	7	3	1	4	2
3	5	1	8	4	2	6	9	7
4	7	2	6	9	1	3	5	8

Medium Puzzle 163

9	3	2	7	5	8	6	4	1
5	8	1	6	4	9	2	7	3
6	7	4	2	1	3	5	8	9
1	4	9	3	7	5	8	2	6
2	6	3	1	8	4	9	5	7
7	5	8	9	6	2	3	1	4
3	1	5	8	9	7	4	6	2
8	9	7	4	2	6	1	3	5
4	2	6	5	3	1	7	9	8

Medium Puzzle 164

7	4	1	8	9	2	5	3	6
8	6	9	7	5	3	1	4	2
5	2	3	6	1	4	7	9	8
6	9	4	1	2	7	8	5	3
2	3	8	5	6	9	4	1	7
1	7	5	4	3	8	2	6	9
3	8	2	9	4	1	6	7	5
4	5	7	3	8	6	9	2	1
9	1	6	2	7	5	3	8	4

Medium Puzzle 165

8	3	1	6	5	4	2	7	9
5	4	2	8	9	7	1	3	6
9	6	7	2	3	1	8	4	5
3	7	9	5	4	2	6	8	1
6	5	8	9	1	3	4	2	7
1	2	4	7	8	6	9	5	3
2	8	5	3	6	9	7	1	4
4	9	3	1	7	8	5	6	2
7	1	6	4	2	5	3	9	8

Medium Puzzle 166

9	4	2	1	7	8	5	6	3
1	7	8	5	6	3	2	9	4
5	6	3	9	2	4	8	7	1
3	9	6	4	8	1	7	2	5
7	2	5	6	3	9	4	1	8
4	8	1	2	5	7	6	3	9
2	1	4	8	9	6	3	5	7
6	3	9	7	4	5	1	8	2
8	5	7	3	1	2	9	4	6

Medium Puzzle 167

1	8	6	9	3	7	5	4	2
3	7	2	4	1	5	6	8	9
9	4	5	6	8	2	1	3	7
2	6	4	5	9	1	8	7	3
5	9	3	7	4	8	2	6	1
7	1	8	2	6	3	4	9	5
4	3	7	1	2	6	9	5	8
8	2	9	3	5	4	7	1	6
6	5	1	8	7	9	3	2	4

Medium Puzzle 168

2	9	7	3	6	1	8	4	5
5	4	1	8	2	7	3	9	6
6	3	8	4	9	5	2	7	1
3	8	5	9	4	2	1	6	7
4	1	6	7	3	8	9	5	2
9	7	2	5	1	6	4	8	3
1	6	9	2	7	4	5	3	8
8	2	4	6	5	3	7	1	9
7	5	3	1	8	9	6	2	4

Medium Puzzle 169

8	5	4	9	3	7	2	6	1
7	9	6	8	2	1	4	5	3
1	3	2	4	6	5	8	7	9
6	2	1	7	4	9	5	3	8
5	7	3	6	1	8	9	2	4
4	8	9	3	5	2	7	1	6
9	6	7	2	8	3	1	4	5
3	1	8	5	7	4	6	9	2
2	4	5	1	9	6	3	8	7

Medium Puzzle 170

5	8	6	3	9	7	1	4	2
4	9	1	2	8	5	7	3	6
3	2	7	1	6	4	5	8	9
7	3	8	5	2	6	4	9	1
6	1	5	7	4	9	3	2	8
9	4	2	8	3	1	6	5	7
1	7	3	9	5	8	2	6	4
8	5	4	6	1	2	9	7	3
2	6	9	4	7	3	8	1	5

Medium Puzzle 171

8	1	5	6	7	3	9	4	2
3	9	2	8	4	5	1	7	6
7	6	4	2	1	9	8	5	3
2	3	7	4	6	8	5	9	1
1	8	9	5	3	2	4	6	7
4	5	6	1	9	7	3	2	8
6	2	3	9	8	4	7	1	5
5	4	8	7	2	1	6	3	9
9	7	1	3	5	6	2	8	4

Medium Puzzle 172

1	9	7	4	3	6	5	2	8
3	8	4	2	5	7	6	1	9
2	5	6	9	8	1	4	3	7
9	3	2	5	6	4	7	8	1
5	4	1	7	9	8	3	6	2
7	6	8	1	2	3	9	5	4
8	7	5	3	4	2	1	9	6
4	2	3	6	1	9	8	7	5
6	1	9	8	7	5	2	4	3

Medium Puzzle 173

6	4	9	1	8	7	2	5	3
5	2	7	6	9	3	8	4	1
8	3	1	5	2	4	6	7	9
2	6	4	7	3	5	1	9	8
9	7	8	2	4	1	3	6	5
1	5	3	8	6	9	4	2	7
3	1	5	4	7	6	9	8	2
7	8	6	9	1	2	5	3	4
4	9	2	3	5	8	7	1	6

Medium Puzzle 174

1	7	6	2	8	5	4	3	9
4	3	8	1	7	9	2	6	5
2	5	9	6	4	3	7	1	8
9	6	1	7	2	8	3	5	4
8	4	7	3	5	1	6	9	2
5	2	3	4	9	6	1	8	7
6	8	2	5	3	4	9	7	1
3	9	4	8	1	7	5	2	6
7	1	5	9	6	2	8	4	3

Medium Puzzle 175

1	8	7	6	4	3	2	9	5
3	4	9	5	2	7	1	8	6
2	6	5	1	9	8	7	4	3
7	3	4	8	6	5	9	2	1
8	9	6	3	1	2	5	7	4
5	2	1	4	7	9	3	6	8
9	1	3	2	8	4	6	5	7
6	7	8	9	5	1	4	3	2
4	5	2	7	3	6	8	1	9

Medium Puzzle 176

3	2	1	4	5	7	8	6	9
6	4	7	9	8	3	2	1	5
9	8	5	1	6	2	3	7	4
7	5	6	3	9	1	4	8	2
4	9	8	5	2	6	7	3	1
2	1	3	8	7	4	5	9	6
8	6	4	2	3	9	1	5	7
1	3	9	7	4	5	6	2	8
5	7	2	6	1	8	9	4	3

Medium Puzzle 177

5	4	1	9	3	8	2	7	6
6	7	2	1	5	4	9	8	3
9	8	3	6	2	7	1	4	5
4	5	9	2	6	1	7	3	8
3	1	6	7	8	9	5	2	4
8	2	7	5	4	3	6	1	9
1	3	5	8	9	2	4	6	7
7	6	8	4	1	5	3	9	2
2	9	4	3	7	6	8	5	1

Medium Puzzle 178

1	2	4	7	3	6	8	9	5
3	9	8	5	2	4	7	6	1
5	7	6	8	9	1	4	3	2
6	4	9	2	7	5	3	1	8
2	8	1	4	6	3	5	7	9
7	5	3	1	8	9	6	2	4
8	3	5	9	1	7	2	4	6
4	1	7	6	5	2	9	8	3
9	6	2	3	4	8	1	5	7

Medium Puzzle 179

5	1	2	3	4	6	7	9	8
8	7	9	1	2	5	6	3	4
4	6	3	9	7	8	5	2	1
3	9	8	5	6	4	2	1	7
6	2	7	8	1	9	4	5	3
1	5	4	2	3	7	9	8	6
2	4	5	6	8	1	3	7	9
9	8	6	7	5	3	1	4	2
7	3	1	4	9	2	8	6	5

Medium Puzzle 180

3	6	5	2	7	1	8	4	9
7	8	9	6	3	4	2	1	5
2	4	1	8	9	5	7	6	3
8	2	3	9	1	6	4	5	7
5	7	6	4	2	8	9	3	1
1	9	4	3	5	7	6	2	8
9	5	7	1	4	2	3	8	6
6	1	2	7	8	3	5	9	4
4	3	8	5	6	9	1	7	2

Medium Puzzle 181

5	2	3	1	7	9	4	8	6
1	8	6	4	2	5	3	9	7
9	7	4	8	3	6	5	1	2
3	9	8	2	6	7	1	5	4
7	1	2	3	5	4	9	6	8
6	4	5	9	1	8	2	7	3
4	5	7	6	9	3	8	2	1
2	3	9	7	8	1	6	4	5
8	6	1	5	4	2	7	3	9

Medium Puzzle 182

2	6	9	3	5	7	1	4	8
8	1	7	9	2	4	5	3	6
4	5	3	6	8	1	2	9	7
5	7	6	4	3	9	8	2	1
3	4	8	7	1	2	9	6	5
9	2	1	8	6	5	4	7	3
6	9	5	1	4	3	7	8	2
7	8	2	5	9	6	3	1	4
1	3	4	2	7	8	6	5	9

Medium Puzzle 183

5	3	2	6	8	4	1	7	9
9	7	8	5	2	1	3	6	4
1	6	4	9	7	3	8	5	2
4	9	7	3	1	2	6	8	5
3	8	5	7	6	9	4	2	1
6	2	1	8	4	5	7	9	3
7	1	9	2	3	6	5	4	8
2	4	6	1	5	8	9	3	7
8	5	3	4	9	7	2	1	6

Medium Puzzle 184

9	1	7	8	4	3	5	2	6
2	3	6	5	9	1	8	4	7
4	8	5	6	2	7	1	9	3
7	4	1	3	5	9	2	6	8
5	6	3	2	1	8	4	7	9
8	2	9	7	6	4	3	1	5
1	7	4	9	8	5	6	3	2
6	9	8	4	3	2	7	5	1
3	5	2	1	7	6	9	8	4

Medium Puzzle 185

7	6	1	3	9	4	2	8	5
3	5	4	2	8	6	1	7	9
8	9	2	5	7	1	4	3	6
9	8	7	1	6	5	3	4	2
6	4	5	8	3	2	9	1	7
2	1	3	7	4	9	5	6	8
4	2	8	9	1	7	6	5	3
1	3	9	6	5	8	7	2	4
5	7	6	4	2	3	8	9	1

Medium Puzzle 186

3	5	4	8	2	6	9	1	7
6	7	1	9	5	4	3	2	8
9	2	8	7	1	3	6	4	5
7	9	5	6	8	2	1	3	4
4	3	2	1	7	5	8	9	6
8	1	6	3	4	9	5	7	2
5	6	7	4	9	1	2	8	3
1	8	3	2	6	7	4	5	9
2	4	9	5	3	8	7	6	1

Medium Puzzle 187

3	4	8	6	7	1	5	2	9
2	5	7	9	8	3	6	4	1
9	1	6	5	2	4	7	8	3
4	3	2	8	5	9	1	6	7
7	6	1	3	4	2	8	9	5
5	8	9	1	6	7	2	3	4
8	7	3	4	1	6	9	5	2
1	9	5	2	3	8	4	7	6
6	2	4	7	9	5	3	1	8

Medium Puzzle 188

5	1	3	4	7	9	8	2	6
8	2	6	5	1	3	4	7	9
4	7	9	8	2	6	1	5	3
9	8	7	2	3	4	6	1	5
2	3	1	6	8	5	9	4	7
6	5	4	1	9	7	3	8	2
1	6	2	9	5	8	7	3	4
3	4	5	7	6	1	2	9	8
7	9	8	3	4	2	5	6	1

Medium Puzzle 189

6	5	8	4	1	7	9	3	2
9	7	3	6	8	2	1	5	4
4	1	2	9	3	5	7	6	8
3	4	1	7	2	9	5	8	6
5	8	9	1	6	3	2	4	7
7	2	6	5	4	8	3	1	9
1	9	5	8	7	6	4	2	3
2	6	4	3	9	1	8	7	5
8	3	7	2	5	4	6	9	1

Medium Puzzle 190

7	6	8	1	9	2	5	4	3
4	5	3	6	8	7	1	9	2
1	2	9	3	4	5	6	7	8
2	1	7	9	5	6	8	3	4
3	4	6	7	2	8	9	5	1
9	8	5	4	3	1	7	2	6
6	3	4	5	1	9	2	8	7
8	9	1	2	7	4	3	6	5
5	7	2	8	6	3	4	1	9

Medium Puzzle 191

2	8	4	6	3	1	7	5	9
6	7	1	5	2	9	4	8	3
9	5	3	7	8	4	6	1	2
3	6	5	8	9	2	1	7	4
4	2	8	1	6	7	9	3	5
1	9	7	4	5	3	8	2	6
8	4	6	3	1	5	2	9	7
7	3	2	9	4	8	5	6	1
5	1	9	2	7	6	3	4	8

Medium Puzzle 192

7	1	9	2	8	6	4	5	3
6	3	2	1	4	5	9	7	8
5	4	8	7	9	3	1	2	6
1	6	4	9	3	2	7	8	5
8	9	7	5	6	4	3	1	2
3	2	5	8	1	7	6	9	4
2	7	3	6	5	9	8	4	1
9	8	6	4	2	1	5	3	7
4	5	1	3	7	8	2	6	9

Medium Puzzle 193

3	5	8	4	9	2	6	1	7
2	4	6	5	1	7	8	3	9
1	9	7	3	6	8	2	5	4
4	7	1	2	5	6	9	8	3
8	3	5	9	4	1	7	2	6
6	2	9	8	7	3	1	4	5
7	6	2	1	3	5	4	9	8
9	1	3	7	8	4	5	6	2
5	8	4	6	2	9	3	7	1

Medium Puzzle 194

7	4	6	1	2	3	9	5	8
3	9	1	5	7	8	6	2	4
8	2	5	6	4	9	7	1	3
5	7	2	8	9	1	4	3	6
4	6	8	7	3	2	1	9	5
1	3	9	4	5	6	2	8	7
6	1	3	9	8	4	5	7	2
9	8	7	2	6	5	3	4	1
2	5	4	3	1	7	8	6	9

Medium Puzzle 195

8	2	4	1	6	7	3	5	9
5	9	6	2	8	3	7	1	4
7	1	3	9	4	5	2	6	8
4	8	2	6	7	1	9	3	5
1	3	7	4	5	9	8	2	6
6	5	9	3	2	8	1	4	7
3	6	8	5	9	2	4	7	1
2	7	5	8	1	4	6	9	3
9	4	1	7	3	6	5	8	2

Medium Puzzle 196

9	6	3	1	2	4	8	7	5
7	5	2	9	3	8	4	6	1
1	4	8	7	5	6	3	2	9
5	8	9	3	7	1	6	4	2
3	7	1	4	6	2	5	9	8
6	2	4	5	8	9	1	3	7
4	3	7	2	1	5	9	8	6
8	9	5	6	4	7	2	1	3
2	1	6	8	9	3	7	5	4

Medium Puzzle 197

1	3	2	9	8	4	7	5	6
8	5	4	7	6	3	1	9	2
9	6	7	5	2	1	3	4	8
5	4	3	2	7	6	8	1	9
7	2	1	3	9	8	4	6	5
6	9	8	1	4	5	2	7	3
4	8	5	6	1	2	9	3	7
3	1	9	8	5	7	6	2	4
2	7	6	4	3	9	5	8	1

Medium Puzzle 198

3	2	9	1	6	7	5	4	8
1	8	6	4	9	5	3	2	7
5	7	4	3	8	2	9	1	6
8	5	7	2	4	1	6	3	9
9	4	1	6	7	3	8	5	2
6	3	2	9	5	8	1	7	4
7	6	3	5	2	9	4	8	1
4	1	8	7	3	6	2	9	5
2	9	5	8	1	4	7	6	3

Medium Puzzle 199

4	3	9	2	1	7	5	8	6
1	2	7	6	5	8	9	4	3
8	5	6	3	9	4	1	7	2
6	8	4	5	7	1	2	3	9
9	1	3	4	6	2	7	5	8
2	7	5	8	3	9	6	1	4
3	4	1	7	2	6	8	9	5
5	9	2	1	8	3	4	6	7
7	6	8	9	4	5	3	2	1

Medium Puzzle 200

5	6	8	1	3	4	9	2	7
2	4	9	7	5	6	3	1	8
3	1	7	2	8	9	6	4	5
9	5	6	8	4	7	1	3	2
4	8	2	3	9	1	5	7	6
1	7	3	5	6	2	4	8	9
8	9	4	6	2	3	7	5	1
7	3	5	9	1	8	2	6	4
6	2	1	4	7	5	8	9	3

Medium Puzzle 201

6	8	7	4	9	5	1	3	2
5	1	2	6	3	7	4	8	9
4	3	9	8	1	2	7	6	5
2	6	1	9	5	4	3	7	8
7	9	4	3	2	8	5	1	6
8	5	3	1	7	6	2	9	4
1	2	6	5	8	3	9	4	7
3	4	5	7	6	9	8	2	1
9	7	8	2	4	1	6	5	3

Medium Puzzle 202

9	3	1	6	4	7	8	5	2
2	5	6	9	8	3	7	1	4
7	4	8	5	2	1	9	6	3
6	8	4	7	5	2	1	3	9
1	2	5	4	3	9	6	8	7
3	7	9	1	6	8	4	2	5
5	9	7	2	1	6	3	4	8
4	6	3	8	9	5	2	7	1
8	1	2	3	7	4	5	9	6

Medium Puzzle 203

6	3	9	8	4	1	7	2	5
7	4	1	5	2	3	8	9	6
5	8	2	9	6	7	3	1	4
4	6	8	3	7	9	1	5	2
9	1	5	6	8	2	4	7	3
2	7	3	4	1	5	9	6	8
3	2	7	1	5	4	6	8	9
1	9	6	2	3	8	5	4	7
8	5	4	7	9	6	2	3	1

Medium Puzzle 204

6	4	2	9	8	1	7	5	3
8	1	7	3	5	4	2	6	9
9	3	5	2	6	7	1	8	4
7	9	6	5	1	8	3	4	2
4	5	3	7	2	6	8	9	1
1	2	8	4	9	3	6	7	5
3	7	9	6	4	2	5	1	8
2	8	4	1	7	5	9	3	6
5	6	1	8	3	9	4	2	7

Medium Puzzle 205

9	5	6	8	1	3	2	4	7
4	1	2	9	7	6	5	8	3
3	7	8	2	4	5	9	1	6
7	6	9	3	8	4	1	2	5
5	8	1	7	2	9	3	6	4
2	3	4	6	5	1	7	9	8
6	2	5	4	9	7	8	3	1
8	4	7	1	3	2	6	5	9
1	9	3	5	6	8	4	7	2

Medium Puzzle 206

3	6	1	8	5	2	9	7	4
7	9	8	6	4	1	3	5	2
4	2	5	7	3	9	1	6	8
2	7	4	3	8	5	6	9	1
6	8	9	1	2	7	5	4	3
5	1	3	4	9	6	2	8	7
1	3	6	5	7	8	4	2	9
9	4	7	2	6	3	8	1	5
8	5	2	9	1	4	7	3	6

Medium Puzzle 207

8	5	1	3	2	6	4	9	7
4	3	9	7	1	5	2	6	8
2	6	7	9	4	8	5	1	3
7	1	8	6	5	9	3	4	2
3	2	5	4	8	1	9	7	6
6	9	4	2	3	7	8	5	1
9	4	2	1	7	3	6	8	5
1	8	6	5	9	2	7	3	4
5	7	3	8	6	4	1	2	9

Medium Puzzle 208

1	5	6	3	8	4	7	9	2
4	8	2	1	7	9	3	5	6
3	7	9	5	6	2	8	1	4
5	9	7	2	1	3	4	6	8
2	3	4	6	9	8	1	7	5
8	6	1	7	4	5	2	3	9
9	2	3	4	5	7	6	8	1
7	1	5	8	2	6	9	4	3
6	4	8	9	3	1	5	2	7

Medium Puzzle 209

7	5	2	6	4	8	3	9	1
9	6	4	1	3	2	5	7	8
1	3	8	7	5	9	2	4	6
3	4	7	9	1	6	8	2	5
2	8	9	5	7	3	6	1	4
5	1	6	8	2	4	9	3	7
8	7	3	2	6	1	4	5	9
6	2	5	4	9	7	1	8	3
4	9	1	3	8	5	7	6	2

Medium Puzzle 210

8	2	1	3	9	6	7	5	4
7	9	4	1	8	5	3	2	6
3	6	5	2	4	7	1	8	9
6	4	2	9	7	8	5	1	3
5	3	9	4	2	1	6	7	8
1	7	8	5	6	3	4	9	2
9	8	6	7	5	4	2	3	1
4	5	3	8	1	2	9	6	7
2	1	7	6	3	9	8	4	5

Medium Puzzle 211

8	3	4	7	5	2	1	9	6
7	1	6	3	4	9	2	8	5
5	9	2	8	1	6	4	3	7
1	8	5	6	7	3	9	4	2
3	4	9	1	2	5	6	7	8
2	6	7	4	9	8	3	5	1
4	5	1	2	3	7	8	6	9
6	7	3	9	8	1	5	2	4
9	2	8	5	6	4	7	1	3

Medium Puzzle 212

3	1	7	2	9	5	4	6	8
8	5	9	4	3	6	7	2	1
4	6	2	7	8	1	5	9	3
2	4	3	5	1	7	6	8	9
7	9	1	8	6	2	3	4	5
5	8	6	9	4	3	1	7	2
1	7	8	6	5	9	2	3	4
9	2	5	3	7	4	8	1	6
6	3	4	1	2	8	9	5	7

Medium Puzzle 213

1	9	4	3	5	6	8	7	2
5	8	3	2	4	7	9	1	6
2	7	6	9	1	8	4	3	5
4	1	2	8	7	5	6	9	3
7	3	5	6	2	9	1	4	8
9	6	8	1	3	4	5	2	7
3	4	7	5	8	1	2	6	9
8	2	9	4	6	3	7	5	1
6	5	1	7	9	2	3	8	4

Medium Puzzle 214

8	5	3	2	1	7	9	6	4
7	4	6	8	9	5	3	1	2
1	2	9	6	4	3	5	8	7
9	1	7	5	8	2	4	3	6
3	8	4	9	7	6	1	2	5
2	6	5	1	3	4	8	7	9
6	3	1	4	2	9	7	5	8
5	9	8	7	6	1	2	4	3
4	7	2	3	5	8	6	9	1

Medium Puzzle 215

9	5	7	6	1	4	8	2	3
1	6	3	2	8	7	9	5	4
4	8	2	3	9	5	1	6	7
6	9	4	5	7	8	3	1	2
7	3	8	1	6	2	4	9	5
5	2	1	9	4	3	7	8	6
3	1	9	4	5	6	2	7	8
2	7	6	8	3	1	5	4	9
8	4	5	7	2	9	6	3	1

Medium Puzzle 216

9	4	5	2	3	6	8	1	7
2	1	3	8	9	7	4	6	5
8	7	6	4	1	5	3	9	2
6	2	9	5	8	4	1	7	3
7	5	4	1	2	3	6	8	9
1	3	8	7	6	9	2	5	4
3	6	1	9	5	2	7	4	8
4	9	2	6	7	8	5	3	1
5	8	7	3	4	1	9	2	6

Medium Puzzle 217

3	1	7	6	2	9	4	8	5
4	5	8	3	7	1	6	2	9
2	9	6	8	5	4	3	7	1
1	8	9	2	4	3	7	5	6
7	6	4	1	8	5	9	3	2
5	2	3	9	6	7	8	1	4
8	7	1	4	9	2	5	6	3
6	4	2	5	3	8	1	9	7
9	3	5	7	1	6	2	4	8

Medium Puzzle 218

8	1	2	6	9	5	3	4	7
9	3	5	2	4	7	1	8	6
6	4	7	1	8	3	2	5	9
2	6	4	3	7	9	5	1	8
7	5	8	4	1	2	9	6	3
3	9	1	8	5	6	4	7	2
4	2	6	5	3	8	7	9	1
1	7	3	9	6	4	8	2	5
5	8	9	7	2	1	6	3	4

Medium Puzzle 219

6	5	2	8	4	3	1	9	7
1	9	4	5	7	6	3	2	8
7	8	3	2	1	9	5	6	4
9	3	5	7	6	1	4	8	2
4	2	1	3	9	8	6	7	5
8	7	6	4	5	2	9	1	3
5	1	8	6	2	4	7	3	9
2	6	7	9	3	5	8	4	1
3	4	9	1	8	7	2	5	6

Medium Puzzle 220

1	2	5	8	4	6	7	9	3
6	9	7	5	3	2	4	1	8
8	4	3	1	7	9	6	5	2
2	8	1	4	6	7	5	3	9
5	7	9	3	8	1	2	4	6
4	3	6	2	9	5	1	8	7
9	6	4	7	5	8	3	2	1
3	1	8	6	2	4	9	7	5
7	5	2	9	1	3	8	6	4

Medium Puzzle 221

8	6	4	9	5	3	7	1	2
7	5	9	8	1	2	3	4	6
2	1	3	4	7	6	9	5	8
6	4	5	3	8	7	2	9	1
1	8	2	5	9	4	6	3	7
9	3	7	6	2	1	5	8	4
5	9	1	2	6	8	4	7	3
4	2	8	7	3	9	1	6	5
3	7	6	1	4	5	8	2	9

Medium Puzzle 222

9	1	2	7	4	5	3	8	6
7	8	5	6	1	3	2	9	4
4	3	6	9	8	2	7	1	5
2	7	9	8	5	6	4	3	1
3	5	1	4	2	9	8	6	7
8	6	4	3	7	1	9	5	2
1	2	8	5	3	4	6	7	9
6	4	7	1	9	8	5	2	3
5	9	3	2	6	7	1	4	8

Medium Puzzle 223

8	9	4	2	5	6	3	7	1
5	6	1	3	8	7	9	2	4
7	3	2	1	4	9	6	8	5
6	8	3	5	7	2	1	4	9
1	2	7	4	9	3	5	6	8
9	4	5	6	1	8	7	3	2
4	1	6	8	3	5	2	9	7
2	5	9	7	6	4	8	1	3
3	7	8	9	2	1	4	5	6

Medium Puzzle 224

7	9	8	4	6	2	5	3	1
2	4	3	9	1	5	7	8	6
5	6	1	7	3	8	2	9	4
8	2	9	1	7	6	3	4	5
3	1	5	8	4	9	6	7	2
6	7	4	5	2	3	9	1	8
1	8	2	6	9	7	4	5	3
4	3	7	2	5	1	8	6	9
9	5	6	3	8	4	1	2	7

Medium Puzzle 225

8	4	6	7	1	3	5	2	9
7	5	1	6	9	2	3	4	8
3	9	2	5	8	4	7	1	6
5	1	3	9	6	8	2	7	4
6	2	8	4	7	1	9	5	3
4	7	9	2	3	5	6	8	1
9	6	5	1	4	7	8	3	2
2	3	4	8	5	9	1	6	7
1	8	7	3	2	6	4	9	5

Medium Puzzle 226

2	9	4	3	8	7	1	6	5
1	5	8	9	6	4	3	2	7
7	6	3	1	5	2	4	8	9
4	1	6	8	9	5	2	7	3
3	7	9	4	2	6	8	5	1
8	2	5	7	1	3	9	4	6
5	3	2	6	4	1	7	9	8
6	8	1	2	7	9	5	3	4
9	4	7	5	3	8	6	1	2

Medium Puzzle 227

4	1	2	8	5	3	6	9	7
5	6	9	7	2	4	8	1	3
7	8	3	9	1	6	2	5	4
3	7	5	6	9	1	4	8	2
8	4	6	5	7	2	9	3	1
2	9	1	4	3	8	7	6	5
6	3	4	2	8	5	1	7	9
9	5	8	1	4	7	3	2	6
1	2	7	3	6	9	5	4	8

Medium Puzzle 228

8	5	7	4	6	2	1	3	9
1	3	2	8	9	5	7	6	4
4	6	9	1	3	7	8	5	2
5	9	6	2	7	3	4	8	1
2	7	4	5	1	8	6	9	3
3	8	1	9	4	6	2	7	5
7	4	5	6	2	9	3	1	8
9	1	3	7	8	4	5	2	6
6	2	8	3	5	1	9	4	7

Medium Puzzle 229

3	4	1	5	6	2	7	9	8
8	6	9	1	3	7	2	5	4
5	2	7	4	9	8	1	6	3
1	9	3	8	7	4	5	2	6
2	5	8	6	1	3	9	4	7
4	7	6	2	5	9	8	3	1
7	1	2	3	4	5	6	8	9
9	3	5	7	8	6	4	1	2
6	8	4	9	2	1	3	7	5

Medium Puzzle 230

6	1	8	4	5	3	7	9	2
4	7	2	1	6	9	3	8	5
9	5	3	2	8	7	1	6	4
7	8	6	9	2	5	4	1	3
1	4	5	3	7	8	6	2	9
3	2	9	6	4	1	5	7	8
8	9	7	5	1	4	2	3	6
5	6	1	8	3	2	9	4	7
2	3	4	7	9	6	8	5	1

Medium Puzzle 231

1	2	6	8	7	9	4	5	3
3	5	9	2	6	4	1	8	7
7	4	8	5	1	3	6	9	2
2	6	5	3	9	7	8	4	1
4	3	7	1	8	5	2	6	9
8	9	1	6	4	2	7	3	5
9	1	3	4	2	6	5	7	8
5	8	4	7	3	1	9	2	6
6	7	2	9	5	8	3	1	4

Medium Puzzle 232

5	3	4	8	6	2	1	7	9
8	2	1	9	7	5	4	6	3
6	7	9	4	3	1	2	5	8
7	1	3	2	5	8	9	4	6
2	9	6	3	4	7	5	8	1
4	5	8	6	1	9	3	2	7
3	8	7	5	9	4	6	1	2
1	6	5	7	2	3	8	9	4
9	4	2	1	8	6	7	3	5

Medium Puzzle 233

3	9	1	6	5	7	2	8	4
6	8	4	3	1	2	5	9	7
5	2	7	8	9	4	3	1	6
1	5	2	9	6	3	7	4	8
9	7	8	4	2	5	6	3	1
4	3	6	1	7	8	9	2	5
7	1	3	5	4	9	8	6	2
8	4	5	2	3	6	1	7	9
2	6	9	7	8	1	4	5	3

Medium Puzzle 234

6	3	7	1	4	2	9	5	8
8	9	1	3	6	5	7	2	4
5	2	4	9	8	7	3	6	1
4	8	9	6	2	1	5	7	3
2	1	6	5	7	3	4	8	9
3	7	5	8	9	4	2	1	6
7	5	8	4	3	6	1	9	2
9	4	2	7	1	8	6	3	5
1	6	3	2	5	9	8	4	7

Medium Puzzle 235

9	8	3	7	1	6	2	4	5
5	7	6	2	4	3	1	8	9
4	1	2	5	9	8	6	3	7
8	5	4	3	6	1	7	9	2
3	6	9	8	7	2	5	1	4
1	2	7	9	5	4	8	6	3
2	3	1	4	8	5	9	7	6
7	4	8	6	2	9	3	5	1
6	9	5	1	3	7	4	2	8

Medium Puzzle 236

7	2	6	5	9	3	1	8	4
4	1	5	7	6	8	2	3	9
3	9	8	2	4	1	7	6	5
6	3	1	8	2	4	5	9	7
5	7	9	3	1	6	4	2	8
8	4	2	9	7	5	3	1	6
1	5	4	6	8	2	9	7	3
2	8	7	4	3	9	6	5	1
9	6	3	1	5	7	8	4	2

Medium Puzzle 237

2	5	9	8	1	3	6	7	4
1	7	6	2	9	4	3	5	8
3	8	4	5	7	6	1	2	9
6	9	7	4	5	2	8	1	3
4	2	5	3	8	1	7	9	6
8	3	1	9	6	7	5	4	2
9	1	2	7	3	8	4	6	5
5	6	8	1	4	9	2	3	7
7	4	3	6	2	5	9	8	1

Medium Puzzle 238

1	3	9	4	2	5	7	6	8
5	7	4	8	6	1	2	3	9
8	2	6	7	9	3	5	1	4
2	4	1	9	8	7	3	5	6
3	9	7	1	5	6	4	8	2
6	8	5	3	4	2	9	7	1
9	6	8	5	7	4	1	2	3
7	1	2	6	3	9	8	4	5
4	5	3	2	1	8	6	9	7

Medium Puzzle 239

2	8	3	1	6	4	7	5	9
6	9	4	5	7	3	1	2	8
7	1	5	9	8	2	3	6	4
8	4	6	7	3	9	2	1	5
3	5	7	2	1	8	4	9	6
9	2	1	6	4	5	8	3	7
5	7	8	3	9	1	6	4	2
1	6	2	4	5	7	9	8	3
4	3	9	8	2	6	5	7	1

Medium Puzzle 240

7	8	1	3	9	4	6	5	2
5	3	9	2	1	6	7	4	8
6	2	4	7	8	5	9	1	3
9	1	6	8	2	3	5	7	4
4	7	2	9	5	1	3	8	6
3	5	8	6	4	7	2	9	1
2	4	7	5	3	8	1	6	9
8	6	3	1	7	9	4	2	5
1	9	5	4	6	2	8	3	7

Medium Puzzle 241

1	6	4	5	7	3	8	2	9
8	7	9	6	2	4	5	3	1
3	5	2	8	9	1	7	4	6
9	4	7	3	8	5	6	1	2
5	3	8	2	1	6	9	7	4
2	1	6	9	4	7	3	8	5
4	9	5	1	3	8	2	6	7
7	2	3	4	6	9	1	5	8
6	8	1	7	5	2	4	9	3

Medium Puzzle 242

5	6	3	9	1	8	2	7	4
4	2	7	5	3	6	1	9	8
8	1	9	4	7	2	3	6	5
7	8	1	2	9	3	5	4	6
3	4	6	7	8	5	9	1	2
2	9	5	1	6	4	8	3	7
1	5	2	3	4	7	6	8	9
9	7	8	6	2	1	4	5	3
6	3	4	8	5	9	7	2	1

Medium Puzzle 243

5	6	4	7	9	3	8	2	1
7	8	1	4	2	5	6	9	3
2	9	3	8	6	1	5	7	4
9	2	6	3	7	4	1	5	8
1	4	5	2	8	9	3	6	7
3	7	8	5	1	6	9	4	2
4	5	2	9	3	8	7	1	6
6	3	7	1	5	2	4	8	9
8	1	9	6	4	7	2	3	5

Medium Puzzle 244

4	9	3	2	7	5	8	1	6
5	2	1	8	6	3	4	7	9
6	7	8	4	1	9	3	2	5
3	1	7	6	5	4	9	8	2
2	8	5	7	9	1	6	3	4
9	6	4	3	2	8	1	5	7
7	4	2	1	3	6	5	9	8
8	3	9	5	4	2	7	6	1
1	5	6	9	8	7	2	4	3

Medium Puzzle 245

4	8	2	3	7	5	6	9	1
7	3	9	4	1	6	5	8	2
6	1	5	2	8	9	4	3	7
5	4	8	1	9	3	2	7	6
1	7	3	6	2	8	9	5	4
2	9	6	7	5	4	3	1	8
3	5	4	8	6	1	7	2	9
8	6	7	9	3	2	1	4	5
9	2	1	5	4	7	8	6	3

Medium Puzzle 246

1	6	5	3	2	8	7	4	9
9	7	4	1	6	5	8	2	3
8	3	2	4	9	7	6	1	5
5	2	7	6	1	4	9	3	8
3	9	1	8	7	2	4	5	6
6	4	8	5	3	9	1	7	2
7	8	6	2	5	1	3	9	4
2	1	3	9	4	6	5	8	7
4	5	9	7	8	3	2	6	1

Medium Puzzle 247

3	7	6	8	4	9	1	2	5
1	9	8	5	2	3	4	7	6
5	2	4	1	7	6	9	3	8
8	4	1	7	5	2	3	6	9
2	5	9	6	3	1	7	8	4
6	3	7	9	8	4	5	1	2
4	6	3	2	9	7	8	5	1
7	8	2	4	1	5	6	9	3
9	1	5	3	6	8	2	4	7

Medium Puzzle 248

7	6	9	1	5	3	4	8	2
4	1	3	2	7	8	6	5	9
2	5	8	4	6	9	3	1	7
8	4	5	6	2	7	9	3	1
6	3	2	5	9	1	8	7	4
1	9	7	3	8	4	5	2	6
3	7	6	8	4	2	1	9	5
9	8	4	7	1	5	2	6	3
5	2	1	9	3	6	7	4	8

Medium Puzzle 249

2	5	8	1	3	9	4	7	6
3	9	1	4	6	7	8	5	2
7	6	4	5	8	2	3	1	9
1	4	7	8	9	6	5	2	3
5	3	2	7	1	4	6	9	8
6	8	9	3	2	5	7	4	1
8	7	6	2	5	1	9	3	4
4	1	3	9	7	8	2	6	5
9	2	5	6	4	3	1	8	7

Medium Puzzle 250

1	9	3	8	7	6	5	4	2
2	7	6	5	4	9	3	1	8
8	5	4	3	1	2	6	9	7
4	8	9	1	6	5	7	2	3
5	6	2	7	9	3	1	8	4
3	1	7	4	2	8	9	5	6
9	4	8	6	5	7	2	3	1
7	2	1	9	3	4	8	6	5
6	3	5	2	8	1	4	7	9

Hard Puzzle 1

9	7	6	4	8	3	2	5	1
2	5	8	7	9	1	6	3	4
1	4	3	6	5	2	9	7	8
7	3	5	2	6	8	4	1	9
8	6	1	9	3	4	5	2	7
4	2	9	5	1	7	3	8	6
6	8	2	3	7	9	1	4	5
3	9	7	1	4	5	8	6	2
5	1	4	8	2	6	7	9	3

Hard Puzzle 2

8	3	5	7	4	2	6	1	9
7	9	4	6	5	1	8	3	2
1	6	2	3	9	8	7	4	5
4	1	8	9	7	5	3	2	6
9	5	6	2	8	3	1	7	4
2	7	3	4	1	6	9	5	8
6	2	1	5	3	9	4	8	7
5	8	7	1	6	4	2	9	3
3	4	9	8	2	7	5	6	1

Hard Puzzle 3

9	5	8	1	7	6	3	2	4
7	3	4	2	8	5	1	9	6
2	6	1	9	4	3	5	7	8
8	9	3	5	6	1	7	4	2
4	2	5	8	9	7	6	3	1
6	1	7	3	2	4	8	5	9
5	4	9	6	3	8	2	1	7
1	8	2	7	5	9	4	6	3
3	7	6	4	1	2	9	8	5

Hard Puzzle 4

3	5	2	4	6	9	7	8	1
4	7	6	2	8	1	9	3	5
9	8	1	5	7	3	2	6	4
7	6	3	8	2	5	1	4	9
1	9	5	7	3	4	8	2	6
2	4	8	9	1	6	5	7	3
8	3	4	1	5	2	6	9	7
6	1	7	3	9	8	4	5	2
5	2	9	6	4	7	3	1	8

Hard Puzzle 5

2	8	9	5	1	3	4	6	7
7	3	6	2	4	8	5	9	1
4	1	5	7	9	6	8	2	3
5	9	7	3	8	4	2	1	6
1	2	4	6	7	5	3	8	9
3	6	8	1	2	9	7	4	5
6	4	3	8	5	1	9	7	2
9	7	1	4	3	2	6	5	8
8	5	2	9	6	7	1	3	4

Hard Puzzle 6

4	8	1	3	7	6	2	5	9
5	2	9	8	4	1	3	6	7
6	7	3	2	9	5	1	8	4
3	1	7	5	8	9	4	2	6
2	5	4	6	1	3	7	9	8
8	9	6	7	2	4	5	1	3
9	4	5	1	6	7	8	3	2
7	3	2	9	5	8	6	4	1
1	6	8	4	3	2	9	7	5

Hard Puzzle 7

1	2	6	8	7	4	5	3	9
9	7	4	6	5	3	2	8	1
5	8	3	1	2	9	4	6	7
2	5	8	3	9	6	7	1	4
4	9	1	2	8	7	3	5	6
6	3	7	5	4	1	9	2	8
8	4	5	7	1	2	6	9	3
7	6	2	9	3	8	1	4	5
3	1	9	4	6	5	8	7	2

Hard Puzzle 8

1	2	5	8	4	6	9	7	3
6	3	7	9	1	2	4	8	5
8	9	4	5	7	3	6	2	1
5	1	8	7	6	4	3	9	2
3	7	9	2	5	1	8	6	4
4	6	2	3	9	8	1	5	7
9	4	6	1	2	5	7	3	8
7	5	3	4	8	9	2	1	6
2	8	1	6	3	7	5	4	9

Hard Puzzle 9

3	6	4	2	5	9	1	8	7
9	8	1	3	4	7	2	5	6
2	5	7	8	1	6	4	9	3
8	1	9	7	3	4	5	6	2
4	7	6	5	9	2	3	1	8
5	2	3	6	8	1	7	4	9
6	9	2	1	7	5	8	3	4
7	3	5	4	6	8	9	2	1
1	4	8	9	2	3	6	7	5

Hard Puzzle 10

2	5	7	4	1	8	9	6	3
4	9	3	7	5	6	8	1	2
1	6	8	2	9	3	4	5	7
7	2	5	1	3	4	6	8	9
6	1	4	8	7	9	2	3	5
3	8	9	5	6	2	7	4	1
8	3	1	6	2	7	5	9	4
9	4	2	3	8	5	1	7	6
5	7	6	9	4	1	3	2	8

Hard Puzzle 11

6	7	1	4	3	5	8	2	9
4	8	2	7	9	1	6	5	3
3	5	9	6	2	8	7	4	1
8	9	5	2	1	6	3	7	4
1	3	6	8	4	7	2	9	5
7	2	4	9	5	3	1	8	6
9	1	3	5	7	2	4	6	8
5	6	7	3	8	4	9	1	2
2	4	8	1	6	9	5	3	7

Hard Puzzle 12

8	4	9	5	1	3	2	7	6
3	2	1	6	7	9	4	8	5
7	5	6	4	8	2	1	3	9
6	7	4	8	3	5	9	1	2
2	9	3	1	6	4	7	5	8
1	8	5	2	9	7	6	4	3
9	3	2	7	4	8	5	6	1
5	1	7	3	2	6	8	9	4
4	6	8	9	5	1	3	2	7

Hard Puzzle 13

9	5	7	8	3	1	6	4	2
2	6	4	7	9	5	8	1	3
8	3	1	6	4	2	5	7	9
1	4	3	5	6	7	2	9	8
6	2	8	9	1	3	4	5	7
7	9	5	4	2	8	1	3	6
4	7	9	2	5	6	3	8	1
5	1	2	3	8	9	7	6	4
3	8	6	1	7	4	9	2	5

Hard Puzzle 14

4	3	5	7	6	8	1	9	2
7	2	1	9	4	3	6	8	5
9	8	6	1	2	5	7	4	3
2	9	3	6	7	1	4	5	8
5	1	4	8	3	9	2	7	6
6	7	8	2	5	4	9	3	1
8	4	2	5	9	6	3	1	7
1	6	9	3	8	7	5	2	4
3	5	7	4	1	2	8	6	9

Hard Puzzle 15

4	5	6	9	7	1	2	3	8
2	3	7	5	4	8	6	9	1
1	9	8	3	6	2	7	4	5
6	7	3	2	5	9	1	8	4
8	4	9	1	3	6	5	2	7
5	1	2	4	8	7	3	6	9
7	8	5	6	9	3	4	1	2
3	2	4	8	1	5	9	7	6
9	6	1	7	2	4	8	5	3

Hard Puzzle 16

3	1	4	2	7	6	9	5	8
2	7	8	9	4	5	6	1	3
9	5	6	3	8	1	2	4	7
8	9	5	4	1	3	7	2	6
1	6	2	7	5	9	8	3	4
7	4	3	8	6	2	1	9	5
6	2	7	5	9	4	3	8	1
5	8	9	1	3	7	4	6	2
4	3	1	6	2	8	5	7	9

Hard Puzzle 17

1	5	7	9	6	2	4	3	8
3	8	2	5	1	4	7	6	9
4	9	6	8	3	7	5	1	2
8	1	9	3	7	5	2	4	6
7	3	4	2	9	6	8	5	1
6	2	5	1	4	8	3	9	7
2	4	3	6	8	9	1	7	5
5	6	1	7	2	3	9	8	4
9	7	8	4	5	1	6	2	3

Hard Puzzle 18

3	8	1	7	5	6	4	9	2
9	2	5	3	1	4	7	6	8
4	6	7	8	2	9	1	3	5
8	9	2	5	4	7	3	1	6
7	1	6	2	9	3	8	5	4
5	3	4	1	6	8	9	2	7
1	4	3	6	7	2	5	8	9
6	5	9	4	8	1	2	7	3
2	7	8	9	3	5	6	4	1

Hard Puzzle 19

3	4	1	9	5	2	6	8	7
2	5	6	4	7	8	1	9	3
9	8	7	1	3	6	4	2	5
8	6	3	2	4	5	9	7	1
4	1	5	7	8	9	2	3	6
7	9	2	3	6	1	8	5	4
1	2	4	5	9	3	7	6	8
5	7	8	6	2	4	3	1	9
6	3	9	8	1	7	5	4	2

Hard Puzzle 20

7	3	5	6	2	4	8	1	9
9	6	4	5	1	8	2	7	3
2	8	1	3	9	7	4	5	6
3	9	7	8	5	2	1	6	4
8	1	2	4	6	3	7	9	5
5	4	6	9	7	1	3	8	2
1	7	9	2	3	5	6	4	8
6	2	8	7	4	9	5	3	1
4	5	3	1	8	6	9	2	7

Hard Puzzle 21

4	2	3	5	7	6	9	1	8
9	1	5	3	2	8	4	6	7
6	8	7	9	1	4	5	2	3
5	9	2	6	8	1	7	3	4
3	6	1	7	4	5	8	9	2
8	7	4	2	9	3	1	5	6
1	3	9	4	6	7	2	8	5
2	4	6	8	5	9	3	7	1
7	5	8	1	3	2	6	4	9

Hard Puzzle 22

8	7	6	9	2	1	3	4	5
3	1	2	5	4	6	8	9	7
4	9	5	8	3	7	2	1	6
5	8	1	3	6	2	4	7	9
2	4	7	1	9	8	5	6	3
9	6	3	7	5	4	1	2	8
7	5	4	2	8	9	6	3	1
1	2	8	6	7	3	9	5	4
6	3	9	4	1	5	7	8	2

Hard Puzzle 23

5	2	4	6	1	3	8	7	9
8	6	1	2	7	9	5	4	3
9	7	3	8	4	5	1	6	2
1	5	6	3	9	4	2	8	7
4	9	2	7	8	1	6	3	5
3	8	7	5	2	6	9	1	4
6	4	8	9	5	7	3	2	1
7	3	5	1	6	2	4	9	8
2	1	9	4	3	8	7	5	6

Hard Puzzle 24

2	5	6	7	3	9	4	8	1
3	4	7	1	6	8	5	9	2
8	1	9	4	5	2	7	6	3
6	8	5	3	7	1	2	4	9
4	9	1	8	2	6	3	5	7
7	2	3	9	4	5	6	1	8
9	6	4	2	8	3	1	7	5
5	3	8	6	1	7	9	2	4
1	7	2	5	9	4	8	3	6

Hard Puzzle 25

2	9	1	6	3	7	8	5	4
7	5	3	8	4	1	9	2	6
6	4	8	5	2	9	1	7	3
4	6	5	9	1	2	7	3	8
1	8	7	4	5	3	6	9	2
3	2	9	7	6	8	4	1	5
9	3	4	2	7	6	5	8	1
8	1	6	3	9	5	2	4	7
5	7	2	1	8	4	3	6	9

Hard Puzzle 26

4	5	2	9	8	6	7	1	3
7	3	6	1	5	4	8	9	2
9	1	8	2	3	7	4	6	5
5	8	9	3	2	1	6	4	7
2	6	4	5	7	8	9	3	1
1	7	3	6	4	9	2	5	8
8	4	5	7	6	3	1	2	9
3	9	7	4	1	2	5	8	6
6	2	1	8	9	5	3	7	4

Hard Puzzle 27

8	2	9	4	5	6	1	7	3
6	3	5	2	1	7	4	9	8
4	7	1	3	9	8	6	2	5
3	9	7	8	4	5	2	6	1
1	4	8	6	2	9	3	5	7
5	6	2	1	7	3	9	8	4
2	8	3	5	6	4	7	1	9
7	1	4	9	8	2	5	3	6
9	5	6	7	3	1	8	4	2

Hard Puzzle28

3	4	9	8	6	7	1	2	5
8	7	5	3	1	2	9	4	6
1	2	6	9	4	5	8	3	7
7	9	1	6	2	3	5	8	4
2	6	8	5	7	4	3	9	1
4	5	3	1	9	8	7	6	2
9	3	4	2	5	1	6	7	8
6	1	7	4	8	9	2	5	3
5	8	2	7	3	6	4	1	9

Hard Puzzle 29

8	1	9	3	4	2	5	7	6
2	7	6	1	5	9	3	8	4
3	5	4	8	6	7	1	9	2
7	6	1	5	2	4	9	3	8
4	3	5	9	1	8	6	2	7
9	2	8	6	7	3	4	1	5
1	9	2	4	8	6	7	5	3
6	8	3	7	9	5	2	4	1
5	4	7	2	3	1	8	6	9

Hard Puzzle 30

4	8	2	6	7	9	1	5	3
1	3	7	5	4	8	6	9	2
9	5	6	3	2	1	8	4	7
8	2	5	4	6	7	3	1	9
6	4	3	1	9	5	7	2	8
7	1	9	8	3	2	5	6	4
3	6	8	2	5	4	9	7	1
5	9	4	7	1	3	2	8	6
2	7	1	9	8	6	4	3	5

Hard Puzzle 31

5	3	7	2	4	8	9	6	1
9	6	8	1	3	5	7	4	2
2	4	1	6	7	9	8	3	5
6	9	2	5	1	3	4	7	8
1	7	4	8	9	6	5	2	3
3	8	5	4	2	7	6	1	9
7	1	6	9	5	2	3	8	4
8	2	9	3	6	4	1	5	7
4	5	3	7	8	1	2	9	6

Hard Puzzle 32

7	2	8	9	3	1	4	5	6
9	1	4	6	5	8	2	7	3
3	5	6	7	4	2	8	1	9
1	9	5	2	7	3	6	8	4
2	6	7	5	8	4	3	9	1
8	4	3	1	9	6	7	2	5
5	7	2	4	6	9	1	3	8
4	3	9	8	1	7	5	6	2
6	8	1	3	2	5	9	4	7

Hard Puzzle 33

7	3	6	8	4	2	5	1	9
9	1	4	5	6	7	3	8	2
5	8	2	1	9	3	7	4	6
3	2	8	7	5	4	9	6	1
1	5	9	6	3	8	4	2	7
6	4	7	9	2	1	8	5	3
2	7	1	4	8	9	6	3	5
4	6	3	2	7	5	1	9	8
8	9	5	3	1	6	2	7	4

Hard Puzzle 34

8	6	1	7	2	4	9	3	5
3	5	7	9	6	8	2	1	4
4	9	2	1	3	5	8	7	6
5	7	3	6	1	2	4	8	9
6	1	8	4	5	9	7	2	3
2	4	9	3	8	7	5	6	1
1	8	4	5	7	6	3	9	2
7	3	5	2	9	1	6	4	8
9	2	6	8	4	3	1	5	7

Hard Puzzle 35

2	1	8	3	6	9	4	7	5
4	7	5	8	1	2	3	9	6
3	6	9	7	5	4	8	2	1
8	4	7	2	3	6	5	1	9
6	9	2	1	8	5	7	3	4
5	3	1	9	4	7	6	8	2
1	8	6	4	9	3	2	5	7
9	2	4	5	7	8	1	6	3
7	5	3	6	2	1	9	4	8

Hard Puzzle 36

2	7	4	8	5	3	6	1	9
3	6	9	2	1	4	8	7	5
8	1	5	7	9	6	2	4	3
1	2	3	9	7	8	5	6	4
5	4	8	6	3	1	7	9	2
7	9	6	4	2	5	1	3	8
9	5	2	3	6	7	4	8	1
6	8	1	5	4	9	3	2	7
4	3	7	1	8	2	9	5	6

Hard Puzzle 37

1	2	9	3	5	4	8	7	6
3	5	7	8	9	6	1	2	4
8	4	6	2	1	7	9	3	5
9	1	5	7	6	8	2	4	3
6	3	4	1	2	5	7	9	8
7	8	2	9	4	3	5	6	1
4	6	1	5	7	9	3	8	2
5	9	8	6	3	2	4	1	7
2	7	3	4	8	1	6	5	9

Hard Puzzle 38

6	5	9	7	1	3	2	8	4
4	8	7	9	5	2	3	6	1
2	3	1	8	4	6	7	5	9
1	6	2	4	8	7	9	3	5
5	7	3	1	2	9	8	4	6
9	4	8	6	3	5	1	2	7
8	9	5	3	6	1	4	7	2
7	2	4	5	9	8	6	1	3
3	1	6	2	7	4	5	9	8

Hard Puzzle 39

5	7	2	1	3	6	4	8	9
1	8	6	4	9	5	7	3	2
3	4	9	8	2	7	5	1	6
4	9	7	5	1	3	6	2	8
2	1	5	6	7	8	9	4	3
6	3	8	2	4	9	1	7	5
8	2	1	9	5	4	3	6	7
7	5	4	3	6	2	8	9	1
9	6	3	7	8	1	2	5	4

Hard Puzzle 40

1	3	2	9	5	4	7	8	6
7	8	5	2	3	6	1	4	9
9	6	4	1	8	7	2	5	3
4	9	3	6	7	1	5	2	8
5	1	7	8	2	9	6	3	4
8	2	6	5	4	3	9	1	7
3	4	9	7	1	2	8	6	5
6	5	1	4	9	8	3	7	2
2	7	8	3	6	5	4	9	1

Hard Puzzle 41

2	8	7	4	6	9	5	1	3
6	3	1	2	8	5	7	4	9
4	9	5	1	3	7	8	2	6
1	6	4	5	7	2	3	9	8
9	2	3	8	4	6	1	7	5
7	5	8	3	9	1	4	6	2
8	4	2	6	1	3	9	5	7
3	7	6	9	5	4	2	8	1
5	1	9	7	2	8	6	3	4

Hard Puzzle 42

7	8	4	2	3	1	6	9	5
6	2	1	7	5	9	4	8	3
5	9	3	4	6	8	1	2	7
3	4	8	1	2	7	5	6	9
9	1	6	5	8	3	7	4	2
2	7	5	9	4	6	3	1	8
1	6	7	3	9	2	8	5	4
4	3	2	8	1	5	9	7	6
8	5	9	6	7	4	2	3	1

Hard Puzzle 43

9	4	6	1	5	2	7	3	8
5	8	1	9	3	7	6	4	2
7	3	2	6	4	8	5	1	9
1	9	3	7	6	5	2	8	4
2	7	5	4	8	1	9	6	3
8	6	4	3	2	9	1	7	5
3	1	8	2	9	6	4	5	7
6	5	9	8	7	4	3	2	1
4	2	7	5	1	3	8	9	6

Hard Puzzle 44

9	5	6	1	8	4	7	3	2
8	7	3	9	6	2	4	1	5
2	4	1	7	5	3	9	6	8
4	3	5	6	7	9	2	8	1
6	8	7	2	4	1	3	5	9
1	2	9	5	3	8	6	4	7
3	1	8	4	9	7	5	2	6
5	9	4	8	2	6	1	7	3
7	6	2	3	1	5	8	9	4

Hard Puzzle 45

7	9	8	3	6	4	1	5	2
3	4	5	7	2	1	6	8	9
1	6	2	5	8	9	7	3	4
6	2	1	9	3	8	4	7	5
4	8	7	2	5	6	3	9	1
5	3	9	1	4	7	2	6	8
9	7	3	8	1	2	5	4	6
2	5	6	4	9	3	8	1	7
8	1	4	6	7	5	9	2	3

Hard Puzzle 46

3	9	6	4	1	2	7	8	5
2	1	8	7	3	5	9	6	4
4	5	7	8	9	6	3	2	1
9	4	5	3	6	8	2	1	7
7	6	2	9	5	1	4	3	8
8	3	1	2	7	4	5	9	6
6	2	9	1	4	7	8	5	3
1	7	3	5	8	9	6	4	2
5	8	4	6	2	3	1	7	9

Hard Puzzle 47

8	6	3	7	1	4	2	9	5
9	1	7	2	5	3	8	6	4
4	5	2	8	9	6	1	7	3
1	2	5	6	7	9	3	4	8
6	3	8	1	4	2	7	5	9
7	4	9	3	8	5	6	1	2
2	7	4	5	6	8	9	3	1
5	8	6	9	3	1	4	2	7
3	9	1	4	2	7	5	8	6

Hard Puzzle 48

6	3	8	5	2	7	1	4	9
9	1	5	6	8	4	7	3	2
2	7	4	9	1	3	6	8	5
5	6	7	2	3	8	9	1	4
8	9	1	4	5	6	3	2	7
3	4	2	1	7	9	5	6	8
7	8	9	3	6	2	4	5	1
1	2	3	7	4	5	8	9	6
4	5	6	8	9	1	2	7	3

Hard Puzzle 49

6	1	4	5	8	7	9	3	2
5	9	8	1	2	3	6	4	7
3	2	7	9	6	4	5	1	8
9	8	2	3	7	5	1	6	4
7	3	1	4	9	6	2	8	5
4	6	5	8	1	2	3	7	9
1	4	9	6	5	8	7	2	3
8	7	6	2	3	9	4	5	1
2	5	3	7	4	1	8	9	6

Hard Puzzle 50

3	2	5	6	9	7	1	8	4
9	1	7	2	8	4	5	3	6
4	8	6	1	3	5	7	2	9
2	4	1	7	5	9	3	6	8
6	7	9	3	1	8	4	5	2
5	3	8	4	6	2	9	7	1
1	6	4	8	7	3	2	9	5
7	5	2	9	4	6	8	1	3
8	9	3	5	2	1	6	4	7

Hard Puzzle 51

1	5	2	4	6	9	7	3	8
7	8	4	2	3	5	6	1	9
3	6	9	1	7	8	5	4	2
8	1	7	6	9	3	2	5	4
6	2	5	7	1	4	9	8	3
4	9	3	8	5	2	1	6	7
9	4	1	3	2	6	8	7	5
2	3	6	5	8	7	4	9	1
5	7	8	9	4	1	3	2	6

Hard Puzzle 52

2	6	9	4	8	5	3	1	7
7	8	4	3	6	1	9	2	5
3	1	5	7	2	9	6	4	8
8	4	2	9	3	7	1	5	6
9	5	6	1	4	2	8	7	3
1	3	7	8	5	6	2	9	4
6	9	1	5	7	3	4	8	2
4	7	3	2	1	8	5	6	9
5	2	8	6	9	4	7	3	1

Hard Puzzle 53

7	2	3	1	8	9	5	4	6
9	4	1	7	6	5	2	8	3
5	6	8	4	2	3	9	1	7
8	9	2	3	1	4	6	7	5
3	5	6	8	7	2	4	9	1
1	7	4	9	5	6	3	2	8
4	3	7	5	9	1	8	6	2
2	1	5	6	4	8	7	3	9
6	8	9	2	3	7	1	5	4

Hard Puzzle 54

7	9	5	2	3	8	1	6	4
1	8	4	6	9	7	5	2	3
2	3	6	1	4	5	8	7	9
9	5	2	7	6	4	3	8	1
6	4	1	8	5	3	2	9	7
3	7	8	9	1	2	6	4	5
4	1	9	5	8	6	7	3	2
8	2	3	4	7	1	9	5	6
5	6	7	3	2	9	4	1	8

Hard Puzzle 55

3	1	9	4	8	7	2	5	6
8	5	6	9	3	2	4	7	1
7	2	4	6	5	1	8	9	3
5	8	7	2	4	3	1	6	9
4	3	2	1	9	6	7	8	5
9	6	1	8	7	5	3	2	4
2	4	3	7	6	9	5	1	8
6	7	5	3	1	8	9	4	2
1	9	8	5	2	4	6	3	7

Hard Puzzle 56

5	9	1	3	7	4	8	2	6
8	4	2	1	5	6	7	3	9
7	6	3	9	8	2	4	1	5
4	3	5	7	6	9	1	8	2
1	7	6	2	3	8	9	5	4
2	8	9	4	1	5	6	7	3
9	1	4	5	2	7	3	6	8
6	2	7	8	9	3	5	4	1
3	5	8	6	4	1	2	9	7

Hard Puzzle 57

7	3	1	6	4	9	2	5	8
8	2	6	7	1	5	9	4	3
4	9	5	8	3	2	7	6	1
3	1	9	4	8	7	6	2	5
5	4	2	9	6	1	8	3	7
6	7	8	2	5	3	1	9	4
2	6	4	5	7	8	3	1	9
1	5	7	3	9	6	4	8	2
9	8	3	1	2	4	5	7	6

Hard Puzzle 58

9	2	3	1	4	8	6	5	7
7	4	1	3	5	6	9	2	8
5	6	8	2	7	9	4	3	1
2	7	4	6	1	5	8	9	3
1	9	5	4	8	3	7	6	2
3	8	6	7	9	2	5	1	4
8	3	9	5	2	4	1	7	6
4	1	2	9	6	7	3	8	5
6	5	7	8	3	1	2	4	9

Hard Puzzle 59

3	2	6	8	4	5	1	7	9
7	9	8	1	2	3	6	4	5
5	4	1	7	9	6	8	2	3
8	5	2	6	7	9	3	1	4
9	7	4	3	1	8	2	5	6
6	1	3	4	5	2	7	9	8
2	3	9	5	8	1	4	6	7
1	8	7	9	6	4	5	3	2
4	6	5	2	3	7	9	8	1

Hard Puzzle 60

3	1	9	4	2	6	7	5	8
5	8	2	1	9	7	3	4	6
4	6	7	5	3	8	9	2	1
6	7	4	2	1	5	8	9	3
8	5	1	3	7	9	4	6	2
9	2	3	8	6	4	5	1	7
7	4	6	9	8	2	1	3	5
2	3	5	7	4	1	6	8	9
1	9	8	6	5	3	2	7	4

Hard Puzzle 61

6	5	7	1	3	8	4	2	9
2	3	1	9	6	4	8	7	5
4	9	8	7	5	2	1	3	6
7	1	5	2	8	6	3	9	4
8	2	4	3	9	7	6	5	1
9	6	3	4	1	5	7	8	2
3	7	6	5	4	9	2	1	8
5	8	2	6	7	1	9	4	3
1	4	9	8	2	3	5	6	7

Hard Puzzle 62

9	1	6	3	7	5	4	2	8
5	8	7	4	9	2	1	3	6
2	3	4	8	1	6	5	7	9
1	7	9	6	5	4	3	8	2
3	5	8	7	2	1	9	6	4
6	4	2	9	3	8	7	5	1
7	6	5	2	4	9	8	1	3
8	9	3	1	6	7	2	4	5
4	2	1	5	8	3	6	9	7

Hard Puzzle 63

6	7	2	4	5	8	9	1	3
4	1	8	3	7	9	6	5	2
9	5	3	2	6	1	8	7	4
5	9	6	8	2	4	1	3	7
8	2	7	1	3	5	4	6	9
3	4	1	7	9	6	2	8	5
7	3	4	6	8	2	5	9	1
2	8	5	9	1	7	3	4	6
1	6	9	5	4	3	7	2	8

Hard Puzzle 64

1	6	8	5	9	7	3	2	4
9	4	3	1	6	2	8	5	7
2	5	7	8	3	4	6	1	9
6	7	1	9	5	3	4	8	2
5	2	4	6	7	8	9	3	1
3	8	9	2	4	1	7	6	5
8	9	6	4	2	5	1	7	3
4	3	5	7	1	6	2	9	8
7	1	2	3	8	9	5	4	6

Hard Puzzle 65

4	3	8	5	6	1	7	2	9
1	9	6	8	2	7	3	5	4
2	5	7	9	3	4	6	1	8
8	7	4	3	1	2	9	6	5
3	2	5	7	9	6	8	4	1
9	6	1	4	8	5	2	7	3
5	8	2	6	4	3	1	9	7
7	1	9	2	5	8	4	3	6
6	4	3	1	7	9	5	8	2

Hard Puzzle 66

2	4	8	9	3	5	1	7	6
1	3	9	6	4	7	8	5	2
7	6	5	8	2	1	9	3	4
3	9	1	2	7	4	5	6	8
4	2	6	5	8	9	3	1	7
5	8	7	1	6	3	2	4	9
8	5	3	4	9	6	7	2	1
6	1	2	7	5	8	4	9	3
9	7	4	3	1	2	6	8	5

Hard Puzzle 67

1	2	5	9	7	3	6	8	4
6	9	3	4	2	8	5	1	7
8	4	7	6	1	5	2	3	9
5	7	2	3	8	9	1	4	6
3	1	4	5	6	2	7	9	8
9	8	6	1	4	7	3	5	2
7	5	9	2	3	4	8	6	1
2	3	1	8	9	6	4	7	5
4	6	8	7	5	1	9	2	3

Hard Puzzle 68

8	3	4	7	2	5	9	6	1
2	7	6	9	1	3	8	4	5
1	5	9	4	6	8	7	2	3
4	6	2	8	3	1	5	9	7
9	8	3	5	7	4	2	1	6
5	1	7	6	9	2	3	8	4
6	9	8	1	5	7	4	3	2
7	2	1	3	4	9	6	5	8
3	4	5	2	8	6	1	7	9

Hard Puzzle 69

5	4	1	8	6	9	2	3	7
7	3	8	4	2	5	9	1	6
9	6	2	1	7	3	8	5	4
1	8	7	9	4	2	5	6	3
6	5	4	7	3	8	1	2	9
3	2	9	6	5	1	4	7	8
8	7	6	5	1	4	3	9	2
2	9	5	3	8	6	7	4	1
4	1	3	2	9	7	6	8	5

Hard Puzzle 70

6	3	8	5	4	9	1	2	7
9	7	4	1	2	6	3	5	8
2	1	5	7	3	8	6	4	9
5	9	1	3	8	4	7	6	2
4	8	2	6	7	5	9	1	3
7	6	3	2	9	1	5	8	4
8	5	7	9	6	2	4	3	1
1	4	9	8	5	3	2	7	6
3	2	6	4	1	7	8	9	5

Hard Puzzle 71

8	6	2	7	3	1	4	9	5
3	7	9	5	6	4	2	1	8
1	5	4	9	2	8	6	3	7
9	1	5	4	8	7	3	6	2
7	3	6	1	5	2	8	4	9
2	4	8	3	9	6	5	7	1
4	8	1	6	7	5	9	2	3
6	2	3	8	1	9	7	5	4
5	9	7	2	4	3	1	8	6

Hard Puzzle 72

1	7	8	2	5	4	9	3	6
3	9	4	7	6	8	2	1	5
6	2	5	3	9	1	8	4	7
4	3	7	9	8	5	6	2	1
8	1	6	4	2	7	3	5	9
2	5	9	6	1	3	7	8	4
9	4	1	8	7	2	5	6	3
7	8	3	5	4	6	1	9	2
5	6	2	1	3	9	4	7	8

Hard Puzzle 73

6	1	3	5	9	2	7	8	4
5	2	7	6	4	8	3	9	1
4	9	8	1	3	7	6	2	5
3	7	6	4	8	1	2	5	9
1	5	2	3	6	9	4	7	8
8	4	9	7	2	5	1	3	6
9	3	1	8	7	6	5	4	2
7	8	5	2	1	4	9	6	3
2	6	4	9	5	3	8	1	7

Hard Puzzle 74

8	4	9	6	1	3	7	2	5
3	1	2	7	9	5	6	4	8
5	6	7	8	4	2	9	3	1
9	3	1	5	8	4	2	7	6
7	2	6	9	3	1	5	8	4
4	8	5	2	6	7	3	1	9
6	7	3	4	5	8	1	9	2
1	5	8	3	2	9	4	6	7
2	9	4	1	7	6	8	5	3

Hard Puzzle 75

5	7	4	6	1	2	9	8	3
3	2	8	7	4	9	1	5	6
9	6	1	5	8	3	7	2	4
1	8	5	4	6	7	2	3	9
7	3	6	9	2	8	4	1	5
2	4	9	3	5	1	8	6	7
6	1	7	2	3	4	5	9	8
4	5	2	8	9	6	3	7	1
8	9	3	1	7	5	6	4	2

Hard Puzzle 76

1	9	8	5	4	3	2	6	7
3	5	7	8	2	6	4	9	1
6	4	2	1	7	9	5	8	3
5	2	6	7	3	1	9	4	8
9	8	1	4	6	5	7	3	2
7	3	4	2	9	8	1	5	6
2	7	3	6	5	4	8	1	9
4	1	9	3	8	7	6	2	5
8	6	5	9	1	2	3	7	4

Hard Puzzle 77

5	4	9	1	8	3	6	7	2
2	6	3	7	5	9	4	1	8
7	1	8	4	2	6	5	9	3
9	2	4	6	3	8	1	5	7
3	5	1	9	7	4	2	8	6
6	8	7	5	1	2	3	4	9
8	9	6	2	4	5	7	3	1
1	3	5	8	6	7	9	2	4
4	7	2	3	9	1	8	6	5

Hard Puzzle 78

3	7	6	9	4	8	1	2	5
5	8	2	7	1	3	6	9	4
1	9	4	6	5	2	3	7	8
6	2	8	1	3	4	9	5	7
4	3	9	5	7	6	2	8	1
7	5	1	2	8	9	4	6	3
9	4	7	3	2	5	8	1	6
2	1	3	8	6	7	5	4	9
8	6	5	4	9	1	7	3	2

Hard Puzzle 79

5	2	8	4	6	7	1	9	3
4	3	9	2	1	8	7	5	6
1	7	6	3	5	9	8	4	2
6	9	7	1	3	5	2	8	4
3	1	5	8	2	4	9	6	7
2	8	4	7	9	6	3	1	5
8	6	1	5	7	2	4	3	9
7	5	3	9	4	1	6	2	8
9	4	2	6	8	3	5	7	1

Hard Puzzle 80

3	9	5	1	7	6	8	2	4
8	4	2	5	3	9	7	1	6
6	7	1	2	4	8	3	9	5
7	1	9	6	8	5	4	3	2
5	3	6	4	1	2	9	8	7
4	2	8	3	9	7	5	6	1
2	6	3	8	5	4	1	7	9
1	5	7	9	6	3	2	4	8
9	8	4	7	2	1	6	5	3

Hard Puzzle 81

8	1	9	7	6	4	3	5	2
6	5	3	1	8	2	9	4	7
7	2	4	5	3	9	1	8	6
1	7	6	8	2	3	5	9	4
4	3	2	6	9	5	8	7	1
9	8	5	4	1	7	6	2	3
3	9	1	2	7	8	4	6	5
2	4	8	3	5	6	7	1	9
5	6	7	9	4	1	2	3	8

Hard Puzzle 82

4	2	6	7	8	5	1	9	3
8	5	9	4	3	1	7	2	6
1	3	7	9	2	6	4	5	8
5	7	8	2	1	4	3	6	9
9	1	3	5	6	7	2	8	4
2	6	4	8	9	3	5	7	1
6	9	5	1	4	2	8	3	7
7	8	1	3	5	9	6	4	2
3	4	2	6	7	8	9	1	5

Hard Puzzle 83

1	3	4	5	9	8	7	6	2
7	6	8	2	1	3	9	4	5
9	5	2	6	7	4	1	3	8
6	2	5	1	3	9	8	7	4
4	8	9	7	6	2	3	5	1
3	1	7	4	8	5	6	2	9
5	9	6	3	4	1	2	8	7
8	4	3	9	2	7	5	1	6
2	7	1	8	5	6	4	9	3

Hard Puzzle 84

3	2	4	8	1	9	7	6	5
6	8	7	2	4	5	1	9	3
5	9	1	7	6	3	8	2	4
4	3	2	9	5	1	6	7	8
9	6	5	4	7	8	2	3	1
7	1	8	6	3	2	4	5	9
1	4	9	3	2	7	5	8	6
8	7	6	5	9	4	3	1	2
2	5	3	1	8	6	9	4	7

Hard Puzzle 85

2	4	3	9	8	1	7	6	5
7	9	1	5	4	6	2	3	8
5	8	6	2	3	7	1	9	4
1	6	8	4	5	3	9	7	2
3	5	7	1	9	2	8	4	6
9	2	4	6	7	8	3	5	1
4	3	5	8	1	9	6	2	7
6	1	9	7	2	4	5	8	3
8	7	2	3	6	5	4	1	9

Hard Puzzle 86

4	1	5	7	2	9	6	8	3
6	7	9	8	5	3	4	1	2
2	3	8	4	6	1	5	7	9
9	8	6	2	1	5	3	4	7
7	5	1	3	4	6	2	9	8
3	2	4	9	8	7	1	5	6
1	4	7	6	9	2	8	3	5
5	6	3	1	7	8	9	2	4
8	9	2	5	3	4	7	6	1

Hard Puzzle 87

4	8	2	1	7	9	5	6	3
6	5	7	3	4	2	8	1	9
1	3	9	8	5	6	2	7	4
2	6	3	4	9	7	1	8	5
9	1	4	5	6	8	3	2	7
5	7	8	2	1	3	4	9	6
8	9	5	6	2	4	7	3	1
3	4	6	7	8	1	9	5	2
7	2	1	9	3	5	6	4	8

Hard Puzzle 88

1	9	4	5	3	7	2	6	8
7	8	6	1	9	2	4	5	3
5	2	3	4	6	8	9	7	1
3	1	8	2	4	6	7	9	5
2	6	7	8	5	9	3	1	4
9	4	5	3	7	1	6	8	2
6	5	2	9	1	4	8	3	7
8	7	1	6	2	3	5	4	9
4	3	9	7	8	5	1	2	6

Hard Puzzle 89

7	6	3	5	9	2	8	1	4
4	2	1	3	8	7	5	6	9
9	8	5	4	1	6	2	3	7
5	1	2	6	7	4	9	8	3
6	9	7	8	2	3	1	4	5
3	4	8	1	5	9	7	2	6
1	3	9	7	4	8	6	5	2
8	7	4	2	6	5	3	9	1
2	5	6	9	3	1	4	7	8

Hard Puzzle 90

1	5	4	6	7	8	2	9	3
6	3	2	9	1	4	5	7	8
7	8	9	3	5	2	6	4	1
8	6	7	1	2	5	4	3	9
2	9	1	4	6	3	8	5	7
3	4	5	7	8	9	1	6	2
4	7	8	2	3	6	9	1	5
5	1	6	8	9	7	3	2	4
9	2	3	5	4	1	7	8	6

Hard Puzzle 91

1	3	7	8	6	2	5	4	9
2	4	8	5	9	1	7	6	3
9	5	6	7	3	4	1	2	8
6	9	5	2	4	7	8	3	1
7	8	2	3	1	9	6	5	4
4	1	3	6	5	8	2	9	7
8	7	4	9	2	5	3	1	6
5	6	1	4	7	3	9	8	2
3	2	9	1	8	6	4	7	5

Hard Puzzle 92

6	3	4	2	8	7	1	5	9
9	7	8	5	6	1	3	4	2
1	5	2	3	4	9	7	6	8
4	6	1	9	7	2	5	8	3
8	2	5	4	3	6	9	1	7
7	9	3	1	5	8	6	2	4
2	4	6	7	1	3	8	9	5
3	8	9	6	2	5	4	7	1
5	1	7	8	9	4	2	3	6

Hard Puzzle 93

2	9	3	8	5	1	6	7	4
8	4	6	3	9	7	2	5	1
5	7	1	6	4	2	8	9	3
6	8	7	9	2	3	4	1	5
3	2	5	1	7	4	9	6	8
9	1	4	5	6	8	7	3	2
7	3	9	4	8	5	1	2	6
4	5	2	7	1	6	3	8	9
1	6	8	2	3	9	5	4	7

Hard Puzzle 94

4	1	6	9	8	5	3	2	7
9	7	5	3	1	2	6	8	4
2	8	3	4	6	7	1	9	5
3	5	8	2	4	1	9	7	6
6	4	9	5	7	3	8	1	2
7	2	1	8	9	6	4	5	3
1	3	4	7	2	9	5	6	8
8	9	2	6	5	4	7	3	1
5	6	7	1	3	8	2	4	9

Hard Puzzle 95

6	1	4	3	8	7	2	9	5
2	7	8	9	6	5	3	4	1
5	3	9	1	2	4	6	7	8
3	8	1	7	4	2	9	5	6
4	9	5	6	1	3	7	8	2
7	2	6	8	5	9	4	1	3
9	5	7	2	3	8	1	6	4
1	4	3	5	7	6	8	2	9
8	6	2	4	9	1	5	3	7

Hard Puzzle 96

9	2	3	6	1	8	4	7	5
8	6	7	2	4	5	9	3	1
5	1	4	9	7	3	2	6	8
7	5	6	1	2	9	3	8	4
4	8	1	5	3	7	6	9	2
2	3	9	8	6	4	5	1	7
1	4	8	3	9	2	7	5	6
6	9	2	7	5	1	8	4	3
3	7	5	4	8	6	1	2	9

Hard Puzzle 97

1	8	6	4	3	5	7	9	2
7	2	4	9	8	6	3	5	1
5	9	3	2	7	1	6	4	8
4	7	8	3	1	2	5	6	9
3	1	9	6	5	4	2	8	7
2	6	5	7	9	8	4	1	3
9	4	1	5	2	7	8	3	6
8	5	2	1	6	3	9	7	4
6	3	7	8	4	9	1	2	5

Hard Puzzle 98

7	2	5	8	6	3	9	4	1
3	8	4	1	9	5	2	6	7
9	6	1	7	2	4	3	8	5
1	5	6	2	8	7	4	9	3
4	3	9	5	1	6	7	2	8
8	7	2	4	3	9	1	5	6
5	4	3	9	7	8	6	1	2
6	1	8	3	4	2	5	7	9
2	9	7	6	5	1	8	3	4

Hard Puzzle 99

6	2	4	5	7	9	8	1	3
5	1	7	6	8	3	2	4	9
3	8	9	4	1	2	6	5	7
8	6	3	9	4	1	5	7	2
4	9	2	7	3	5	1	6	8
7	5	1	2	6	8	9	3	4
1	3	6	8	2	7	4	9	5
9	7	8	1	5	4	3	2	6
2	4	5	3	9	6	7	8	1

Hard Puzzle 100

7	4	6	8	9	3	2	5	1
8	2	9	1	4	5	6	7	3
1	3	5	6	7	2	9	8	4
9	1	4	2	6	8	5	3	7
5	7	2	9	3	4	1	6	8
3	6	8	7	5	1	4	9	2
6	5	1	3	2	7	8	4	9
4	8	7	5	1	9	3	2	6
2	9	3	4	8	6	7	1	5

Hard Puzzle 101

1	3	8	4	5	2	7	6	9
6	4	9	7	3	8	5	1	2
5	2	7	9	6	1	3	4	8
2	6	3	8	9	5	1	7	4
7	8	1	6	2	4	9	3	5
4	9	5	3	1	7	8	2	6
9	1	2	5	4	3	6	8	7
3	7	6	2	8	9	4	5	1
8	5	4	1	7	6	2	9	3

Hard Puzzle 102

8	4	5	1	3	6	2	9	7
2	6	9	4	8	7	1	5	3
7	1	3	5	2	9	8	6	4
9	3	4	8	5	2	7	1	6
5	7	1	9	6	3	4	2	8
6	2	8	7	1	4	5	3	9
1	5	6	3	4	8	9	7	2
4	9	2	6	7	1	3	8	5
3	8	7	2	9	5	6	4	1

Hard Puzzle 103

8	6	1	5	7	9	3	2	4
2	9	4	6	8	3	5	1	7
7	5	3	4	1	2	9	6	8
4	3	2	8	9	1	6	7	5
9	8	6	7	3	5	2	4	1
5	1	7	2	6	4	8	3	9
1	4	8	3	5	6	7	9	2
6	7	9	1	2	8	4	5	3
3	2	5	9	4	7	1	8	6

Hard Puzzle 104

6	4	8	1	7	9	5	3	2
2	9	5	8	3	6	4	7	1
7	1	3	5	2	4	8	9	6
5	3	7	4	8	1	6	2	9
8	6	1	2	9	3	7	4	5
4	2	9	6	5	7	3	1	8
3	8	4	9	6	2	1	5	7
9	7	6	3	1	5	2	8	4
1	5	2	7	4	8	9	6	3

Hard Puzzle 105

5	3	7	6	9	2	1	8	4
8	1	2	3	4	5	7	9	6
6	9	4	1	8	7	5	2	3
2	8	6	9	5	1	3	4	7
3	7	1	8	6	4	9	5	2
4	5	9	7	2	3	8	6	1
7	4	8	5	1	6	2	3	9
1	6	5	2	3	9	4	7	8
9	2	3	4	7	8	6	1	5

Hard Puzzle 106

5	8	7	6	2	1	4	9	3
6	2	1	4	9	3	5	7	8
9	4	3	8	5	7	6	1	2
2	9	5	3	8	4	1	6	7
8	3	6	1	7	5	9	2	4
7	1	4	9	6	2	3	8	5
4	7	9	2	3	6	8	5	1
3	6	2	5	1	8	7	4	9
1	5	8	7	4	9	2	3	6

Hard Puzzle 107

7	1	3	4	9	5	8	2	6
4	6	8	1	3	2	7	9	5
9	2	5	6	8	7	3	1	4
1	8	7	2	4	3	6	5	9
6	9	2	5	1	8	4	7	3
3	5	4	9	7	6	1	8	2
8	7	6	3	2	9	5	4	1
2	3	1	7	5	4	9	6	8
5	4	9	8	6	1	2	3	7

Hard Puzzle 108

7	6	5	1	9	8	3	4	2
4	2	3	5	7	6	8	1	9
1	9	8	2	3	4	5	7	6
8	3	6	4	2	7	1	9	5
9	1	7	6	5	3	4	2	8
2	5	4	8	1	9	7	6	3
5	7	2	9	8	1	6	3	4
6	8	1	3	4	2	9	5	7
3	4	9	7	6	5	2	8	1

Hard Puzzle 109

2	9	4	3	1	8	7	5	6
8	1	6	4	7	5	2	9	3
5	3	7	6	9	2	1	4	8
7	6	9	5	4	3	8	1	2
3	8	2	1	6	9	4	7	5
1	4	5	2	8	7	3	6	9
4	2	8	9	5	1	6	3	7
9	7	1	8	3	6	5	2	4
6	5	3	7	2	4	9	8	1

Hard Puzzle 110

1	5	3	2	6	8	9	4	7
6	4	7	5	3	9	2	8	1
8	2	9	4	7	1	6	5	3
2	7	8	6	9	5	1	3	4
5	6	1	8	4	3	7	2	9
9	3	4	1	2	7	8	6	5
4	1	2	9	5	6	3	7	8
3	8	5	7	1	2	4	9	6
7	9	6	3	8	4	5	1	2

Hard Puzzle 111

5	6	7	3	4	1	2	9	8
3	4	9	8	6	2	7	5	1
8	2	1	7	9	5	3	6	4
4	3	8	5	7	6	1	2	9
1	7	5	2	8	9	4	3	6
6	9	2	4	1	3	8	7	5
9	8	4	6	2	7	5	1	3
2	1	3	9	5	8	6	4	7
7	5	6	1	3	4	9	8	2

Hard Puzzle 112

1	3	4	2	7	6	8	5	9
7	8	5	9	4	1	6	3	2
6	9	2	8	5	3	1	7	4
3	1	9	6	8	5	4	2	7
5	4	6	7	1	2	9	8	3
8	2	7	4	3	9	5	1	6
2	5	3	1	6	4	7	9	8
4	7	1	3	9	8	2	6	5
9	6	8	5	2	7	3	4	1

Hard Puzzle 113

9	6	4	8	5	2	3	1	7
3	8	1	4	9	7	2	5	6
7	5	2	3	1	6	4	8	9
8	9	3	6	4	1	5	7	2
2	4	5	9	7	8	6	3	1
6	1	7	5	2	3	9	4	8
1	7	9	2	3	5	8	6	4
5	2	6	7	8	4	1	9	3
4	3	8	1	6	9	7	2	5

Hard Puzzle 114

1	4	6	7	9	5	2	8	3
2	8	9	6	4	3	5	1	7
3	5	7	8	1	2	9	4	6
7	2	1	3	8	9	4	6	5
6	9	4	5	2	7	1	3	8
8	3	5	1	6	4	7	2	9
5	1	2	9	3	6	8	7	4
4	7	3	2	5	8	6	9	1
9	6	8	4	7	1	3	5	2

Hard Puzzle 115

1	7	6	5	3	4	8	9	2
4	8	2	6	9	1	3	7	5
5	9	3	7	8	2	4	1	6
6	2	7	3	1	9	5	8	4
3	1	8	4	2	5	9	6	7
9	4	5	8	7	6	1	2	3
7	5	9	2	4	8	6	3	1
8	3	4	1	6	7	2	5	9
2	6	1	9	5	3	7	4	8

Hard Puzzle 116

2	8	3	5	9	1	4	7	6
6	1	4	2	3	7	9	8	5
5	7	9	8	4	6	1	2	3
7	6	8	4	1	9	3	5	2
3	9	1	6	2	5	7	4	8
4	5	2	3	7	8	6	9	1
9	2	6	7	5	3	8	1	4
8	4	7	1	6	2	5	3	9
1	3	5	9	8	4	2	6	7

Hard Puzzle 117

5	6	4	2	7	8	3	9	1
8	2	1	3	9	6	4	5	7
9	7	3	4	5	1	6	2	8
3	1	8	6	2	5	7	4	9
7	4	6	8	3	9	2	1	5
2	5	9	7	1	4	8	6	3
4	9	7	1	8	2	5	3	6
1	3	2	5	6	7	9	8	4
6	8	5	9	4	3	1	7	2

Hard Puzzle 118

6	2	4	3	9	1	5	8	7
1	3	7	6	8	5	9	2	4
9	8	5	4	2	7	3	1	6
3	4	9	8	5	2	7	6	1
8	5	2	1	7	6	4	9	3
7	1	6	9	3	4	2	5	8
4	6	3	2	1	9	8	7	5
5	9	8	7	6	3	1	4	2
2	7	1	5	4	8	6	3	9

Hard Puzzle 119

1	4	8	7	6	9	3	2	5
5	3	6	1	8	2	7	9	4
9	7	2	3	5	4	8	6	1
4	8	5	6	2	3	9	1	7
3	2	1	4	9	7	5	8	6
6	9	7	5	1	8	2	4	3
8	5	4	2	7	6	1	3	9
2	1	3	9	4	5	6	7	8
7	6	9	8	3	1	4	5	2

Hard Puzzle 120

7	2	4	3	9	5	8	6	1
5	8	9	1	6	4	2	3	7
6	1	3	2	8	7	5	9	4
8	7	1	4	2	3	6	5	9
3	5	2	6	7	9	1	4	8
4	9	6	5	1	8	7	2	3
1	6	8	9	3	2	4	7	5
9	4	7	8	5	6	3	1	2
2	3	5	7	4	1	9	8	6

Hard Puzzle 121

6	8	2	4	3	1	9	5	7
3	1	7	9	5	2	8	6	4
9	5	4	6	8	7	2	3	1
5	3	6	8	1	9	4	7	2
7	4	9	5	2	6	3	1	8
8	2	1	3	7	4	5	9	6
1	9	8	7	4	5	6	2	3
2	6	3	1	9	8	7	4	5
4	7	5	2	6	3	1	8	9

Hard Puzzle 122

4	3	9	5	2	6	1	8	7
6	2	7	8	1	4	9	3	5
5	8	1	3	7	9	4	2	6
1	9	5	2	4	3	7	6	8
3	6	2	7	9	8	5	4	1
7	4	8	6	5	1	2	9	3
9	5	6	4	8	7	3	1	2
2	1	3	9	6	5	8	7	4
8	7	4	1	3	2	6	5	9

Hard Puzzle 123

1	3	5	2	9	4	8	6	7
6	2	4	5	7	8	1	3	9
8	9	7	6	3	1	5	2	4
4	1	6	9	8	7	2	5	3
7	5	3	1	6	2	4	9	8
2	8	9	3	4	5	6	7	1
5	4	1	7	2	3	9	8	6
9	7	2	8	1	6	3	4	5
3	6	8	4	5	9	7	1	2

Hard Puzzle 124

4	1	2	9	7	8	6	3	5
7	5	9	6	3	2	4	1	8
6	3	8	4	5	1	2	7	9
3	8	7	2	4	5	9	6	1
9	4	6	8	1	7	5	2	3
1	2	5	3	6	9	8	4	7
5	6	4	1	9	3	7	8	2
8	7	3	5	2	4	1	9	6
2	9	1	7	8	6	3	5	4

Hard Puzzle 125

2	6	1	5	3	8	7	4	9
7	4	5	9	2	6	8	1	3
9	8	3	4	1	7	2	5	6
4	7	9	6	8	5	1	3	2
3	5	2	1	9	4	6	8	7
6	1	8	3	7	2	4	9	5
1	9	7	2	4	3	5	6	8
5	2	4	8	6	9	3	7	1
8	3	6	7	5	1	9	2	4

Hard Puzzle 126

5	3	2	8	9	4	1	6	7
8	4	6	7	5	1	9	2	3
7	9	1	3	6	2	5	4	8
1	2	4	9	7	5	8	3	6
6	7	8	1	4	3	2	5	9
3	5	9	6	2	8	7	1	4
4	1	3	2	8	7	6	9	5
2	6	7	5	3	9	4	8	1
9	8	5	4	1	6	3	7	2

Hard Puzzle 127

5	7	9	1	4	2	6	3	8
6	1	4	3	8	9	7	5	2
8	2	3	7	5	6	4	9	1
7	8	2	4	3	1	5	6	9
9	4	5	2	6	8	1	7	3
3	6	1	9	7	5	2	8	4
4	5	8	6	2	3	9	1	7
1	3	7	5	9	4	8	2	6
2	9	6	8	1	7	3	4	5

Hard Puzzle 128

2	9	5	6	7	1	3	8	4
4	1	6	2	3	8	9	5	7
3	7	8	9	4	5	6	2	1
9	3	2	7	1	4	8	6	5
8	6	1	3	5	9	7	4	2
7	5	4	8	2	6	1	9	3
1	8	3	4	6	2	5	7	9
6	4	7	5	9	3	2	1	8
5	2	9	1	8	7	4	3	6

Hard Puzzle 129

1	5	4	6	3	9	2	7	8
3	7	2	4	5	8	1	6	9
9	6	8	1	2	7	4	3	5
8	9	6	2	1	4	3	5	7
5	1	7	9	8	3	6	2	4
2	4	3	7	6	5	8	9	1
4	3	1	5	7	2	9	8	6
6	8	5	3	9	1	7	4	2
7	2	9	8	4	6	5	1	3

Hard Puzzle 130

3	2	1	4	7	6	8	9	5
8	4	5	3	2	9	6	7	1
6	7	9	8	1	5	4	3	2
5	1	6	9	4	8	7	2	3
4	8	3	7	5	2	9	1	6
7	9	2	6	3	1	5	4	8
9	3	8	2	6	7	1	5	4
1	6	4	5	9	3	2	8	7
2	5	7	1	8	4	3	6	9

Hard Puzzle 131

7	2	8	4	1	6	3	9	5
3	9	4	8	5	2	7	1	6
1	5	6	3	9	7	4	2	8
2	8	3	5	4	1	9	6	7
6	4	9	7	2	3	5	8	1
5	7	1	6	8	9	2	3	4
9	6	5	2	7	8	1	4	3
8	1	7	9	3	4	6	5	2
4	3	2	1	6	5	8	7	9

Hard Puzzle 132

6	9	8	5	4	2	7	1	3
3	5	7	6	9	1	8	4	2
2	1	4	7	8	3	5	9	6
4	2	9	1	7	5	3	6	8
1	6	3	4	2	8	9	5	7
7	8	5	9	3	6	4	2	1
8	3	1	2	5	4	6	7	9
9	4	6	3	1	7	2	8	5
5	7	2	8	6	9	1	3	4

Hard Puzzle 133

3	4	2	8	7	9	5	1	6
1	7	9	5	3	6	8	2	4
8	6	5	1	4	2	7	9	3
4	2	6	3	1	7	9	5	8
9	1	3	2	8	5	6	4	7
5	8	7	6	9	4	1	3	2
6	9	4	7	2	1	3	8	5
2	5	8	9	6	3	4	7	1
7	3	1	4	5	8	2	6	9

Hard Puzzle 134

1	6	8	7	9	3	4	5	2
9	5	4	1	2	6	3	7	8
2	7	3	4	8	5	9	6	1
7	8	2	9	3	4	5	1	6
3	9	1	6	5	2	7	8	4
6	4	5	8	1	7	2	9	3
5	3	7	2	6	8	1	4	9
8	2	9	5	4	1	6	3	7
4	1	6	3	7	9	8	2	5

Hard Puzzle 135

7	1	8	9	5	4	3	2	6
2	9	5	8	6	3	7	1	4
4	3	6	2	7	1	8	5	9
6	5	4	7	3	2	1	9	8
3	8	7	5	1	9	6	4	2
1	2	9	6	4	8	5	7	3
5	6	2	3	9	7	4	8	1
8	4	3	1	2	5	9	6	7
9	7	1	4	8	6	2	3	5

Hard Puzzle 136

2	7	1	8	9	3	5	4	6
5	3	9	1	6	4	2	7	8
8	6	4	2	5	7	1	9	3
4	2	6	7	3	1	9	8	5
7	9	5	6	4	8	3	1	2
3	1	8	5	2	9	4	6	7
9	4	7	3	8	5	6	2	1
6	8	3	4	1	2	7	5	9
1	5	2	9	7	6	8	3	4

Hard Puzzle 137

9	4	1	3	8	7	6	2	5
3	2	8	6	1	5	9	7	4
6	7	5	9	2	4	3	1	8
5	3	7	2	4	6	1	8	9
8	6	4	1	3	9	7	5	2
2	1	9	7	5	8	4	3	6
4	9	3	5	7	2	8	6	1
7	8	2	4	6	1	5	9	3
1	5	6	8	9	3	2	4	7

Hard Puzzle 138

6	7	9	2	1	3	5	8	4
3	8	1	4	7	5	2	9	6
2	4	5	8	9	6	7	3	1
8	5	4	6	3	2	9	1	7
7	1	3	9	4	8	6	2	5
9	6	2	7	5	1	3	4	8
1	3	7	5	2	4	8	6	9
5	2	8	1	6	9	4	7	3
4	9	6	3	8	7	1	5	2

Hard Puzzle 139

5	4	7	3	6	9	1	8	2
2	3	9	5	1	8	4	6	7
8	1	6	4	7	2	5	3	9
4	2	5	8	9	7	3	1	6
6	7	8	1	5	3	9	2	4
3	9	1	6	2	4	8	7	5
7	8	2	9	4	1	6	5	3
1	5	4	7	3	6	2	9	8
9	6	3	2	8	5	7	4	1

Hard Puzzle 140

3	9	4	1	5	2	6	8	7
2	7	5	6	8	3	9	4	1
6	8	1	4	9	7	5	3	2
5	6	3	2	7	4	1	9	8
4	1	7	9	6	8	2	5	3
8	2	9	5	3	1	7	6	4
7	4	6	3	1	9	8	2	5
1	5	2	8	4	6	3	7	9
9	3	8	7	2	5	4	1	6

Hard Puzzle 141

6	4	2	7	8	9	3	1	5
5	3	1	4	2	6	8	7	9
9	8	7	3	5	1	2	6	4
4	7	6	1	3	5	9	8	2
2	9	5	6	7	8	1	4	3
3	1	8	2	9	4	6	5	7
7	5	3	8	6	2	4	9	1
8	2	4	9	1	7	5	3	6
1	6	9	5	4	3	7	2	8

Hard Puzzle 142

9	3	4	6	5	8	1	7	2
8	1	5	2	4	7	9	3	6
6	7	2	3	1	9	4	8	5
5	4	3	7	2	1	8	6	9
7	6	1	9	8	3	2	5	4
2	8	9	4	6	5	3	1	7
1	2	7	8	9	6	5	4	3
4	5	6	1	3	2	7	9	8
3	9	8	5	7	4	6	2	1

Hard Puzzle 143

6	7	8	2	9	3	1	4	5
2	9	3	5	4	1	7	6	8
5	4	1	8	7	6	3	2	9
3	8	2	9	6	5	4	1	7
1	5	7	4	3	8	6	9	2
9	6	4	1	2	7	8	5	3
7	1	5	6	8	2	9	3	4
4	3	6	7	5	9	2	8	1
8	2	9	3	1	4	5	7	6

Hard Puzzle 144

9	7	3	5	2	6	1	4	8
1	4	2	8	3	7	5	9	6
5	6	8	1	4	9	3	2	7
3	5	1	7	9	2	6	8	4
8	2	4	3	6	1	7	5	9
7	9	6	4	8	5	2	3	1
4	1	9	2	7	3	8	6	5
6	3	5	9	1	8	4	7	2
2	8	7	6	5	4	9	1	3

Hard Puzzle 145

2	5	6	4	7	3	9	1	8
7	3	8	6	1	9	4	5	2
1	4	9	2	5	8	3	7	6
9	7	2	5	3	6	8	4	1
4	1	5	8	2	7	6	3	9
8	6	3	9	4	1	7	2	5
6	2	7	1	8	4	5	9	3
3	8	1	7	9	5	2	6	4
5	9	4	3	6	2	1	8	7

Hard Puzzle 146

7	2	6	1	4	8	5	3	9
5	8	1	9	2	3	7	6	4
3	4	9	6	7	5	1	8	2
4	1	3	5	9	6	8	2	7
8	7	5	2	3	4	6	9	1
9	6	2	8	1	7	4	5	3
6	9	4	3	8	1	2	7	5
1	3	8	7	5	2	9	4	6
2	5	7	4	6	9	3	1	8

Hard Puzzle 147

5	4	6	3	7	8	2	1	9
7	8	1	9	6	2	5	4	3
3	9	2	4	5	1	7	6	8
1	5	7	8	3	9	6	2	4
4	6	3	7	2	5	9	8	1
9	2	8	1	4	6	3	7	5
6	1	5	2	8	3	4	9	7
8	3	4	6	9	7	1	5	2
2	7	9	5	1	4	8	3	6

Hard Puzzle 148

2	4	7	1	6	9	8	5	3
9	3	8	4	2	5	1	6	7
6	5	1	7	8	3	2	4	9
8	6	4	5	3	7	9	1	2
3	9	2	6	4	1	7	8	5
1	7	5	8	9	2	4	3	6
7	8	3	2	1	6	5	9	4
5	1	6	9	7	4	3	2	8
4	2	9	3	5	8	6	7	1

Hard Puzzle 149

5	3	1	9	8	4	6	7	2
6	9	7	3	5	2	4	8	1
4	8	2	1	7	6	5	3	9
2	6	3	4	9	7	1	5	8
1	4	8	5	2	3	7	9	6
9	7	5	6	1	8	2	4	3
8	2	4	7	6	9	3	1	5
3	5	6	8	4	1	9	2	7
7	1	9	2	3	5	8	6	4

Hard Puzzle 150

1	9	8	7	6	4	2	3	5
4	7	5	3	8	2	9	6	1
3	6	2	1	5	9	8	4	7
5	3	7	2	4	1	6	9	8
8	1	4	6	9	5	3	7	2
9	2	6	8	7	3	5	1	4
2	4	1	5	3	6	7	8	9
6	8	9	4	2	7	1	5	3
7	5	3	9	1	8	4	2	6

Hard Puzzle 151

6	1	2	7	8	9	3	4	5
4	8	9	1	3	5	6	2	7
3	7	5	2	6	4	9	8	1
7	9	8	5	4	2	1	3	6
2	6	3	8	9	1	7	5	4
5	4	1	3	7	6	8	9	2
1	2	6	9	5	8	4	7	3
9	5	7	4	1	3	2	6	8
8	3	4	6	2	7	5	1	9

Hard Puzzle 152

3	6	1	2	7	8	9	5	4
7	2	4	5	9	1	6	3	8
8	9	5	6	4	3	7	2	1
4	7	6	9	3	5	8	1	2
9	5	8	1	2	4	3	6	7
1	3	2	7	8	6	4	9	5
2	8	3	4	5	9	1	7	6
6	4	7	3	1	2	5	8	9
5	1	9	8	6	7	2	4	3

Hard Puzzle 153

3	9	2	4	8	6	7	5	1
7	1	4	2	5	9	6	3	8
6	8	5	7	3	1	2	9	4
4	3	1	8	9	2	5	6	7
8	7	6	5	1	3	4	2	9
5	2	9	6	4	7	1	8	3
2	4	7	3	6	8	9	1	5
9	6	8	1	7	5	3	4	2
1	5	3	9	2	4	8	7	6

Hard Puzzle 154

4	8	1	3	9	5	2	7	6
3	7	2	4	6	8	1	5	9
9	5	6	7	2	1	3	4	8
2	6	5	8	1	3	7	9	4
1	3	7	5	4	9	6	8	2
8	4	9	2	7	6	5	3	1
7	1	3	6	8	4	9	2	5
6	2	8	9	5	7	4	1	3
5	9	4	1	3	2	8	6	7

Hard Puzzle 155

7	1	8	6	9	2	5	3	4
9	3	2	5	4	8	7	6	1
5	4	6	1	7	3	9	8	2
6	8	1	9	3	5	4	2	7
2	7	9	8	1	4	3	5	6
4	5	3	2	6	7	8	1	9
3	6	5	7	2	9	1	4	8
8	2	7	4	5	1	6	9	3
1	9	4	3	8	6	2	7	5

Hard Puzzle 156

4	9	3	6	8	7	5	1	2
8	1	7	2	5	9	3	6	4
5	6	2	3	1	4	7	8	9
3	2	8	1	9	5	4	7	6
7	4	9	8	2	6	1	5	3
6	5	1	4	7	3	9	2	8
9	8	6	5	4	1	2	3	7
1	3	4	7	6	2	8	9	5
2	7	5	9	3	8	6	4	1

Hard Puzzle 157

1	9	5	4	3	7	2	8	6
4	2	8	9	1	6	3	7	5
3	6	7	2	8	5	9	4	1
5	7	2	8	4	9	6	1	3
9	1	4	5	6	3	8	2	7
8	3	6	7	2	1	5	9	4
6	4	9	3	7	2	1	5	8
7	5	1	6	9	8	4	3	2
2	8	3	1	5	4	7	6	9

Hard Puzzle 158

7	6	2	9	5	1	4	8	3
1	5	9	8	3	4	7	2	6
3	4	8	6	2	7	9	1	5
6	2	5	4	9	8	1	3	7
9	7	3	1	6	2	8	5	4
8	1	4	5	7	3	6	9	2
5	9	7	3	1	6	2	4	8
4	3	6	2	8	9	5	7	1
2	8	1	7	4	5	3	6	9

Hard Puzzle 159

5	3	1	7	9	4	6	2	8
7	4	2	6	8	3	1	5	9
6	8	9	2	1	5	3	4	7
4	7	6	8	2	1	9	3	5
8	2	3	4	5	9	7	6	1
1	9	5	3	6	7	2	8	4
9	6	7	5	3	8	4	1	2
2	1	8	9	4	6	5	7	3
3	5	4	1	7	2	8	9	6

Hard Puzzle 160

9	8	2	3	7	1	4	5	6
4	3	5	6	8	9	1	2	7
6	7	1	4	2	5	3	9	8
8	5	4	7	9	2	6	1	3
7	2	6	1	3	4	9	8	5
1	9	3	8	5	6	2	7	4
3	1	8	9	6	7	5	4	2
2	6	9	5	4	8	7	3	1
5	4	7	2	1	3	8	6	9

Hard Puzzle 161

9	2	8	5	4	6	3	7	1
6	1	5	8	7	3	9	2	4
3	7	4	1	2	9	6	5	8
2	6	3	7	1	8	5	4	9
7	8	9	4	3	5	1	6	2
4	5	1	9	6	2	7	8	3
8	9	2	3	5	7	4	1	6
5	4	6	2	9	1	8	3	7
1	3	7	6	8	4	2	9	5

Hard Puzzle 162

5	1	3	8	2	4	6	7	9
6	8	2	9	7	5	4	3	1
4	9	7	3	1	6	5	8	2
7	6	4	1	8	2	3	9	5
9	5	8	6	3	7	1	2	4
2	3	1	4	5	9	8	6	7
3	7	9	5	4	8	2	1	6
1	2	5	7	6	3	9	4	8
8	4	6	2	9	1	7	5	3

Hard Puzzle 163

9	2	5	7	4	3	8	6	1
3	6	1	9	2	8	5	4	7
7	8	4	1	6	5	3	9	2
4	3	7	2	9	6	1	5	8
6	9	8	3	5	1	2	7	4
5	1	2	4	8	7	6	3	9
1	4	6	8	3	9	7	2	5
8	5	9	6	7	2	4	1	3
2	7	3	5	1	4	9	8	6

Hard Puzzle 164

3	4	7	8	6	5	2	9	1
1	8	6	9	7	2	3	4	5
2	5	9	3	4	1	6	8	7
8	7	5	4	9	3	1	6	2
4	1	2	5	8	6	9	7	3
9	6	3	1	2	7	4	5	8
6	2	1	7	5	9	8	3	4
7	9	4	2	3	8	5	1	6
5	3	8	6	1	4	7	2	9

Hard Puzzle 165

8	7	2	9	1	6	3	4	5
6	9	4	3	7	5	8	2	1
1	5	3	2	8	4	9	6	7
2	3	5	6	9	7	4	1	8
7	4	1	5	3	8	6	9	2
9	8	6	1	4	2	7	5	3
5	6	8	4	2	3	1	7	9
3	2	9	7	6	1	5	8	4
4	1	7	8	5	9	2	3	6

Hard Puzzle 166

3	8	1	2	6	9	5	4	7
4	5	6	1	3	7	8	9	2
7	9	2	4	5	8	3	6	1
1	7	5	3	9	2	4	8	6
8	3	4	6	7	5	2	1	9
6	2	9	8	4	1	7	3	5
5	4	8	7	1	6	9	2	3
9	6	3	5	2	4	1	7	8
2	1	7	9	8	3	6	5	4

Hard Puzzle 167

8	5	6	9	2	7	1	3	4
9	2	3	1	4	8	5	7	6
4	1	7	3	5	6	8	2	9
2	7	4	6	8	5	3	9	1
6	9	8	2	3	1	7	4	5
5	3	1	7	9	4	6	8	2
3	6	9	5	7	2	4	1	8
1	4	2	8	6	3	9	5	7
7	8	5	4	1	9	2	6	3

Hard Puzzle 168

8	5	9	4	6	1	2	7	3
4	3	7	2	9	5	6	8	1
2	6	1	3	8	7	4	5	9
6	1	4	8	2	9	5	3	7
7	9	3	5	4	6	1	2	8
5	8	2	7	1	3	9	6	4
9	2	5	1	7	8	3	4	6
3	7	6	9	5	4	8	1	2
1	4	8	6	3	2	7	9	5

Hard Puzzle 169

6	8	1	9	7	4	3	2	5
3	7	9	5	2	8	1	6	4
2	5	4	1	3	6	9	7	8
7	4	3	6	8	5	2	1	9
5	1	2	4	9	3	7	8	6
8	9	6	2	1	7	5	4	3
9	6	5	7	4	1	8	3	2
1	2	8	3	6	9	4	5	7
4	3	7	8	5	2	6	9	1

Hard Puzzle 170

9	2	4	8	5	6	3	7	1
6	3	1	9	2	7	4	5	8
5	7	8	3	1	4	2	9	6
7	8	3	1	9	2	5	6	4
2	1	6	7	4	5	9	8	3
4	9	5	6	8	3	1	2	7
3	4	9	5	7	8	6	1	2
8	5	2	4	6	1	7	3	9
1	6	7	2	3	9	8	4	5

Hard Puzzle 171

2	5	1	6	3	8	4	9	7
7	6	3	4	9	1	8	2	5
4	9	8	5	2	7	6	3	1
1	7	4	9	6	3	5	8	2
6	2	9	7	8	5	3	1	4
8	3	5	2	1	4	9	7	6
5	8	6	1	7	9	2	4	3
9	1	2	3	4	6	7	5	8
3	4	7	8	5	2	1	6	9

Hard Puzzle 172

3	6	5	2	4	1	7	8	9
4	2	9	8	3	7	5	6	1
1	8	7	9	5	6	3	2	4
8	1	4	5	7	9	2	3	6
5	9	3	6	8	2	4	1	7
6	7	2	3	1	4	8	9	5
2	4	8	1	9	5	6	7	3
9	5	6	7	2	3	1	4	8
7	3	1	4	6	8	9	5	2

Hard Puzzle 173

6	8	9	2	3	1	4	7	5
7	1	4	6	5	8	9	3	2
5	2	3	9	7	4	1	8	6
2	5	8	4	1	3	7	6	9
9	6	1	8	2	7	5	4	3
3	4	7	5	6	9	8	2	1
8	3	5	7	9	6	2	1	4
1	7	2	3	4	5	6	9	8
4	9	6	1	8	2	3	5	7

Hard Puzzle 174

5	1	8	4	2	3	6	9	7
4	3	9	1	6	7	2	5	8
2	7	6	5	8	9	4	3	1
9	5	4	2	3	1	8	7	6
3	6	7	8	9	4	5	1	2
1	8	2	7	5	6	3	4	9
6	2	1	9	4	5	7	8	3
7	4	3	6	1	8	9	2	5
8	9	5	3	7	2	1	6	4

Hard Puzzle 175

4	2	1	5	3	8	7	9	6
6	9	8	7	1	4	5	2	3
5	7	3	9	2	6	8	4	1
8	4	2	3	7	5	6	1	9
3	5	7	1	6	9	4	8	2
9	1	6	4	8	2	3	5	7
1	3	5	2	4	7	9	6	8
2	6	4	8	9	3	1	7	5
7	8	9	6	5	1	2	3	4

Hard Puzzle 176

2	3	5	9	4	1	6	7	8
6	9	1	7	5	8	3	4	2
7	8	4	2	3	6	1	5	9
1	7	8	5	6	4	2	9	3
5	2	3	8	9	7	4	6	1
4	6	9	1	2	3	5	8	7
8	5	6	3	7	2	9	1	4
9	1	2	4	8	5	7	3	6
3	4	7	6	1	9	8	2	5

Hard Puzzle 177

2	3	7	6	9	1	5	8	4
8	4	5	3	2	7	9	1	6
9	6	1	5	8	4	7	3	2
6	1	8	7	5	9	4	2	3
3	5	4	8	6	2	1	7	9
7	2	9	4	1	3	6	5	8
5	9	3	2	7	6	8	4	1
4	7	6	1	3	8	2	9	5
1	8	2	9	4	5	3	6	7

Hard Puzzle 178

8	5	2	3	7	9	4	1	6
3	7	9	4	6	1	8	5	2
6	1	4	2	8	5	7	9	3
4	2	7	8	1	6	5	3	9
1	8	5	9	4	3	2	6	7
9	3	6	5	2	7	1	4	8
5	9	1	7	3	8	6	2	4
2	6	8	1	9	4	3	7	5
7	4	3	6	5	2	9	8	1

Hard Puzzle 179

8	9	5	6	3	2	4	7	1
1	2	6	8	4	7	3	9	5
7	4	3	5	1	9	8	6	2
5	3	8	9	6	4	2	1	7
9	7	1	3	2	8	5	4	6
4	6	2	1	7	5	9	8	3
2	8	7	4	5	6	1	3	9
6	1	4	2	9	3	7	5	8
3	5	9	7	8	1	6	2	4

Hard Puzzle 180

4	9	5	1	2	3	6	8	7
1	2	3	8	6	7	5	4	9
7	6	8	4	9	5	1	3	2
9	3	4	7	5	1	8	2	6
8	1	6	2	4	9	7	5	3
2	5	7	3	8	6	9	1	4
5	8	9	6	3	4	2	7	1
3	7	2	9	1	8	4	6	5
6	4	1	5	7	2	3	9	8

Hard Puzzle 181

5	1	7	9	6	2	8	3	4
6	9	3	5	8	4	1	7	2
8	4	2	1	3	7	6	5	9
4	2	5	3	1	6	9	8	7
7	8	6	4	2	9	5	1	3
1	3	9	8	7	5	4	2	6
9	7	1	2	4	8	3	6	5
2	5	8	6	9	3	7	4	1
3	6	4	7	5	1	2	9	8

Hard Puzzle 182

8	4	9	2	7	1	6	3	5
5	1	2	9	3	6	4	7	8
7	3	6	5	8	4	1	2	9
6	7	3	8	9	2	5	4	1
2	8	1	4	5	7	3	9	6
4	9	5	1	6	3	2	8	7
9	2	4	6	1	8	7	5	3
3	6	8	7	2	5	9	1	4
1	5	7	3	4	9	8	6	2

Hard Puzzle 183

5	6	8	9	7	1	4	2	3
4	3	1	2	6	8	5	7	9
7	9	2	5	3	4	6	1	8
8	2	3	1	9	5	7	4	6
9	7	6	3	4	2	1	8	5
1	5	4	6	8	7	9	3	2
2	8	5	7	1	9	3	6	4
3	1	9	4	2	6	8	5	7
6	4	7	8	5	3	2	9	1

Hard Puzzle 184

1	3	2	8	4	7	5	6	9
6	8	4	5	9	3	1	2	7
5	7	9	1	6	2	8	4	3
7	1	6	3	5	4	9	8	2
2	5	3	6	8	9	4	7	1
4	9	8	2	7	1	6	3	5
9	6	7	4	2	5	3	1	8
8	2	1	9	3	6	7	5	4
3	4	5	7	1	8	2	9	6

Hard Puzzle 185

3	2	7	6	8	1	5	4	9
6	5	1	4	3	9	7	8	2
8	9	4	5	7	2	1	3	6
4	6	9	7	5	8	2	1	3
5	8	2	1	9	3	6	7	4
1	7	3	2	6	4	8	9	5
2	3	6	8	4	7	9	5	1
7	4	5	9	1	6	3	2	8
9	1	8	3	2	5	4	6	7

Hard Puzzle 186

3	2	4	8	1	9	7	6	5
6	8	7	2	4	5	1	9	3
5	9	1	7	6	3	8	2	4
4	3	2	9	5	1	6	7	8
9	6	5	4	7	8	2	3	1
7	1	8	6	3	2	4	5	9
1	4	9	3	2	7	5	8	6
8	7	6	5	9	4	3	1	2
2	5	3	1	8	6	9	4	7

Hard Puzzle 187

7	9	6	3	4	1	2	5	8
5	8	4	9	7	2	1	3	6
3	2	1	8	5	6	7	4	9
8	3	7	6	1	5	4	9	2
2	6	9	7	3	4	5	8	1
4	1	5	2	9	8	3	6	7
9	7	2	5	6	3	8	1	4
6	4	3	1	8	7	9	2	5
1	5	8	4	2	9	6	7	3

Hard Puzzle 188

1	3	7	2	8	9	4	6	5
2	6	4	3	1	5	8	9	7
8	5	9	7	4	6	2	3	1
9	7	8	1	3	2	5	4	6
5	4	3	6	7	8	9	1	2
6	1	2	5	9	4	7	8	3
7	9	6	4	5	1	3	2	8
4	2	5	8	6	3	1	7	9
3	8	1	9	2	7	6	5	4

Hard Puzzle 189

2	5	4	8	1	7	6	9	3
8	6	7	9	5	3	1	4	2
1	9	3	6	2	4	5	8	7
7	8	1	4	6	5	2	3	9
9	2	6	7	3	8	4	5	1
3	4	5	2	9	1	7	6	8
5	1	9	3	4	2	8	7	6
4	3	8	1	7	6	9	2	5
6	7	2	5	8	9	3	1	4

Hard Puzzle 190

7	2	8	9	6	1	5	3	4
5	1	4	7	8	3	9	6	2
3	6	9	5	2	4	8	7	1
1	5	7	3	9	6	4	2	8
2	8	6	4	5	7	3	1	9
4	9	3	2	1	8	7	5	6
9	3	1	8	7	2	6	4	5
6	4	5	1	3	9	2	8	7
8	7	2	6	4	5	1	9	3

Hard Puzzle 191

4	8	6	1	7	2	5	3	9
2	7	9	6	5	3	8	1	4
3	1	5	8	9	4	7	6	2
9	5	3	2	4	7	6	8	1
7	2	8	3	6	1	4	9	5
1	6	4	9	8	5	3	2	7
8	3	7	4	1	9	2	5	6
6	4	1	5	2	8	9	7	3
5	9	2	7	3	6	1	4	8

Hard Puzzle 192

8	6	7	5	3	2	9	4	1
5	3	4	8	1	9	6	2	7
2	1	9	6	7	4	8	3	5
9	2	5	3	4	7	1	6	8
4	7	1	2	6	8	5	9	3
6	8	3	1	9	5	4	7	2
1	9	2	7	5	6	3	8	4
3	4	8	9	2	1	7	5	6
7	5	6	4	8	3	2	1	9

Hard Puzzle 193

1	9	7	8	5	6	3	2	4
3	5	2	9	4	7	1	8	6
8	6	4	2	3	1	5	7	9
6	4	8	7	1	3	2	9	5
9	7	5	6	2	4	8	3	1
2	1	3	5	8	9	4	6	7
5	8	9	1	6	2	7	4	3
7	3	1	4	9	8	6	5	2
4	2	6	3	7	5	9	1	8

Hard Puzzle 194

9	7	2	3	5	4	1	8	6
6	8	4	7	9	1	3	2	5
1	5	3	8	6	2	9	4	7
2	1	6	4	3	8	7	5	9
5	4	9	2	7	6	8	3	1
8	3	7	5	1	9	2	6	4
4	9	5	1	8	3	6	7	2
3	2	1	6	4	7	5	9	8
7	6	8	9	2	5	4	1	3

Hard Puzzle 195

3	7	2	6	1	5	8	9	4
4	5	6	9	2	8	1	7	3
8	1	9	3	4	7	2	5	6
5	2	3	7	8	9	4	6	1
7	8	1	2	6	4	9	3	5
9	6	4	1	5	3	7	8	2
2	3	7	5	9	1	6	4	8
1	4	5	8	7	6	3	2	9
6	9	8	4	3	2	5	1	7

Hard Puzzle 196

2	3	9	6	5	8	7	4	1
8	5	6	7	1	4	9	3	2
7	1	4	9	3	2	8	6	5
6	4	7	1	2	5	3	8	9
3	9	1	4	8	7	2	5	6
5	2	8	3	9	6	1	7	4
4	8	3	2	6	1	5	9	7
1	7	5	8	4	9	6	2	3
9	6	2	5	7	3	4	1	8

Hard Puzzle 197

8	6	5	2	3	1	4	9	7
9	7	3	4	6	8	2	1	5
1	2	4	5	9	7	6	8	3
7	3	1	6	5	2	9	4	8
2	9	6	3	8	4	7	5	1
4	5	8	1	7	9	3	2	6
6	4	7	8	2	5	1	3	9
3	8	2	9	1	6	5	7	4
5	1	9	7	4	3	8	6	2

Hard Puzzle 198

8	4	6	5	3	9	1	7	2
2	5	3	4	7	1	8	6	9
9	1	7	8	2	6	3	5	4
5	3	2	1	6	7	9	4	8
6	8	9	2	4	3	7	1	5
4	7	1	9	5	8	2	3	6
3	2	8	6	1	4	5	9	7
7	6	5	3	9	2	4	8	1
1	9	4	7	8	5	6	2	3

Hard Puzzle 199

1	6	4	9	8	5	2	7	3
5	3	9	2	4	7	6	1	8
8	2	7	3	1	6	4	9	5
2	8	6	7	9	3	1	5	4
4	7	1	8	5	2	3	6	9
9	5	3	4	6	1	7	8	2
6	9	2	5	7	4	8	3	1
7	4	5	1	3	8	9	2	6
3	1	8	6	2	9	5	4	7

Hard Puzzle 200

6	9	3	5	4	2	8	7	1
2	8	5	7	6	1	3	9	4
7	4	1	3	9	8	6	5	2
4	2	7	1	3	9	5	8	6
8	5	9	6	2	7	1	4	3
3	1	6	8	5	4	7	2	9
9	6	8	2	7	3	4	1	5
1	3	4	9	8	5	2	6	7
5	7	2	4	1	6	9	3	8

Hard Puzzle 201

5	4	8	2	6	3	1	9	7
6	1	3	4	7	9	5	8	2
2	7	9	5	1	8	4	6	3
3	5	6	8	9	2	7	4	1
8	2	1	7	4	6	3	5	9
4	9	7	3	5	1	6	2	8
9	3	5	6	8	7	2	1	4
7	8	4	1	2	5	9	3	6
1	6	2	9	3	4	8	7	5

Hard Puzzle 202

8	4	1	9	2	5	3	7	6
7	3	5	6	1	8	4	2	9
6	9	2	4	3	7	1	8	5
1	2	8	3	9	6	5	4	7
9	7	6	5	4	1	2	3	8
3	5	4	8	7	2	6	9	1
2	6	3	7	5	9	8	1	4
4	8	7	1	6	3	9	5	2
5	1	9	2	8	4	7	6	3

Hard Puzzle 203

7	8	3	1	9	2	5	4	6
6	5	9	4	8	7	2	3	1
4	2	1	5	6	3	8	9	7
8	1	6	9	7	4	3	5	2
2	4	7	3	5	8	1	6	9
3	9	5	2	1	6	4	7	8
1	7	4	6	2	5	9	8	3
9	3	8	7	4	1	6	2	5
5	6	2	8	3	9	7	1	4

Hard Puzzle 204

9	4	1	7	6	5	8	2	3
5	2	8	9	4	3	7	1	6
6	3	7	2	1	8	5	9	4
1	8	3	6	5	2	9	4	7
2	5	6	4	7	9	3	8	1
4	7	9	8	3	1	6	5	2
8	6	4	5	2	7	1	3	9
3	9	2	1	8	6	4	7	5
7	1	5	3	9	4	2	6	8

Hard Puzzle 205

8	6	5	1	2	3	9	4	7
2	1	3	4	7	9	6	5	8
7	9	4	8	5	6	2	1	3
5	7	2	6	3	1	4	8	9
6	4	9	2	8	7	5	3	1
1	3	8	9	4	5	7	2	6
3	5	1	7	9	2	8	6	4
9	8	6	5	1	4	3	7	2
4	2	7	3	6	8	1	9	5

Hard Puzzle 206

9	3	7	2	4	8	6	5	1
2	4	5	6	1	7	8	3	9
8	6	1	5	3	9	2	4	7
1	2	3	8	6	5	9	7	4
7	5	4	3	9	2	1	8	6
6	8	9	4	7	1	5	2	3
5	9	6	7	2	3	4	1	8
3	1	8	9	5	4	7	6	2
4	7	2	1	8	6	3	9	5

Hard Puzzle 207

1	8	4	3	2	6	7	9	5
6	7	9	4	5	8	2	1	3
2	5	3	1	7	9	6	4	8
7	2	8	9	1	3	5	6	4
4	3	5	6	8	2	1	7	9
9	1	6	5	4	7	3	8	2
5	9	2	8	6	1	4	3	7
3	6	7	2	9	4	8	5	1
8	4	1	7	3	5	9	2	6

Hard Puzzle 208

6	2	7	9	1	3	8	4	5
5	1	9	7	8	4	6	2	3
8	4	3	6	5	2	7	1	9
7	8	1	4	6	9	3	5	2
2	3	4	5	7	8	1	9	6
9	5	6	2	3	1	4	8	7
1	6	8	3	2	5	9	7	4
3	9	5	1	4	7	2	6	8
4	7	2	8	9	6	5	3	1

Hard Puzzle 209

4	8	2	6	7	9	1	5	3
1	3	7	5	4	8	6	9	2
9	5	6	3	2	1	8	4	7
8	2	5	4	6	7	3	1	9
6	4	3	1	9	5	7	2	8
7	1	9	8	3	2	5	6	4
3	6	8	2	5	4	9	7	1
5	9	4	7	1	3	2	8	6
2	7	1	9	8	6	4	3	5

Hard Puzzle 210

6	5	2	1	8	9	7	4	3
8	1	9	4	3	7	6	2	5
4	3	7	2	6	5	8	9	1
3	7	6	5	2	8	4	1	9
1	2	4	9	7	6	5	3	8
9	8	5	3	4	1	2	6	7
7	4	1	8	9	2	3	5	6
2	9	8	6	5	3	1	7	4
5	6	3	7	1	4	9	8	2

Hard Puzzle 211

5	4	9	8	3	1	2	7	6
3	7	8	5	2	6	1	4	9
2	1	6	4	7	9	5	8	3
8	5	3	2	4	7	9	6	1
6	2	1	9	5	8	4	3	7
7	9	4	6	1	3	8	5	2
1	6	5	3	9	4	7	2	8
4	3	7	1	8	2	6	9	5
9	8	2	7	6	5	3	1	4

Hard Puzzle 212

7	3	9	1	8	4	5	2	6
4	6	1	3	5	2	9	8	7
5	8	2	7	6	9	4	1	3
1	7	5	4	2	8	3	6	9
6	4	3	9	1	7	2	5	8
2	9	8	6	3	5	1	7	4
3	5	4	2	7	6	8	9	1
8	1	7	5	9	3	6	4	2
9	2	6	8	4	1	7	3	5

Hard Puzzle 213

7	8	6	4	5	1	9	3	2
5	4	2	6	9	3	1	8	7
1	9	3	8	7	2	5	4	6
6	3	5	7	1	4	2	9	8
8	1	7	3	2	9	6	5	4
9	2	4	5	6	8	3	7	1
2	7	8	9	3	6	4	1	5
3	5	1	2	4	7	8	6	9
4	6	9	1	8	5	7	2	3

Hard Puzzle 214

8	6	9	2	5	7	1	4	3
4	1	2	6	9	3	8	5	7
5	7	3	4	8	1	9	2	6
2	5	1	7	6	8	3	9	4
7	3	4	1	2	9	5	6	8
6	9	8	3	4	5	7	1	2
1	2	7	9	3	4	6	8	5
9	8	6	5	7	2	4	3	1
3	4	5	8	1	6	2	7	9

Hard Puzzle 215

1	7	9	3	8	6	5	2	4
3	2	5	9	4	1	8	6	7
6	4	8	7	5	2	1	9	3
5	9	7	6	1	3	4	8	2
4	8	1	2	9	5	7	3	6
2	6	3	8	7	4	9	1	5
8	3	4	5	6	9	2	7	1
9	5	2	1	3	7	6	4	8
7	1	6	4	2	8	3	5	9

Hard Puzzle 216

9	6	4	2	8	1	5	7	3
8	2	1	3	7	5	4	6	9
5	7	3	4	6	9	2	1	8
2	8	7	1	9	4	3	5	6
6	1	5	8	3	7	9	4	2
3	4	9	6	5	2	1	8	7
4	5	8	7	2	3	6	9	1
7	9	2	5	1	6	8	3	4
1	3	6	9	4	8	7	2	5

Hard Puzzle 217

1	7	9	6	8	2	5	4	3
2	8	5	7	4	3	6	1	9
6	3	4	5	1	9	2	8	7
8	9	1	2	3	4	7	6	5
5	4	7	9	6	1	8	3	2
3	6	2	8	7	5	4	9	1
4	1	6	3	2	7	9	5	8
7	5	8	1	9	6	3	2	4
9	2	3	4	5	8	1	7	6

Hard Puzzle 218

4	6	8	2	9	7	5	3	1
1	7	9	5	4	3	8	2	6
3	2	5	8	1	6	9	7	4
9	3	2	7	6	1	4	8	5
8	5	1	4	3	2	6	9	7
6	4	7	9	5	8	2	1	3
7	9	3	6	2	4	1	5	8
5	8	4	1	7	9	3	6	2
2	1	6	3	8	5	7	4	9

Hard Puzzle 219

4	9	2	1	8	5	7	6	3
5	3	8	6	2	7	1	9	4
6	7	1	9	4	3	8	5	2
8	1	4	3	7	6	9	2	5
7	6	9	5	1	2	4	3	8
2	5	3	8	9	4	6	1	7
9	4	6	2	3	8	5	7	1
1	2	7	4	5	9	3	8	6
3	8	5	7	6	1	2	4	9

Hard Puzzle 220

6	5	8	7	9	3	1	2	4
3	2	9	1	6	4	5	7	8
7	4	1	2	5	8	9	3	6
2	1	3	8	7	5	6	4	9
4	6	5	3	2	9	7	8	1
8	9	7	6	4	1	2	5	3
9	7	6	4	8	2	3	1	5
5	3	4	9	1	7	8	6	2
1	8	2	5	3	6	4	9	7

Hard Puzzle 221

9	8	3	1	2	4	6	7	5
2	4	6	5	7	9	8	1	3
1	7	5	6	8	3	4	9	2
8	5	1	2	3	6	7	4	9
6	3	9	4	5	7	2	8	1
4	2	7	9	1	8	5	3	6
3	9	4	8	6	2	1	5	7
7	1	2	3	4	5	9	6	8
5	6	8	7	9	1	3	2	4

Hard Puzzle 222

7	1	5	8	9	2	6	4	3
9	8	4	6	1	3	5	2	7
6	2	3	7	4	5	1	8	9
8	3	2	1	5	9	4	7	6
1	5	6	4	7	8	9	3	2
4	7	9	3	2	6	8	5	1
3	9	7	5	6	4	2	1	8
5	6	1	2	8	7	3	9	4
2	4	8	9	3	1	7	6	5

Hard Puzzle 223

7	5	8	3	2	6	1	9	4
3	4	9	1	7	8	2	6	5
6	1	2	9	4	5	7	3	8
2	9	3	6	5	7	4	8	1
4	6	7	8	1	3	9	5	2
1	8	5	2	9	4	6	7	3
8	3	4	7	6	2	5	1	9
5	7	1	4	3	9	8	2	6
9	2	6	5	8	1	3	4	7

Hard Puzzle 224

6	5	9	4	2	7	1	8	3
2	8	7	1	5	3	4	6	9
3	1	4	9	6	8	7	2	5
8	4	1	2	3	9	6	5	7
7	2	3	6	8	5	9	4	1
5	9	6	7	1	4	2	3	8
9	6	8	5	7	2	3	1	4
1	7	5	3	4	6	8	9	2
4	3	2	8	9	1	5	7	6

Hard Puzzle 225

1	7	3	4	8	9	5	2	6
5	6	2	3	1	7	4	8	9
9	8	4	2	6	5	7	1	3
3	9	1	7	5	2	8	6	4
2	4	7	6	3	8	1	9	5
6	5	8	1	9	4	2	3	7
7	2	6	9	4	1	3	5	8
8	1	9	5	7	3	6	4	2
4	3	5	8	2	6	9	7	1

Hard Puzzle 226

7	2	9	4	3	8	6	1	5
6	4	8	9	1	5	3	7	2
5	3	1	7	2	6	8	4	9
1	5	2	8	6	3	7	9	4
8	9	3	1	7	4	5	2	6
4	7	6	2	5	9	1	8	3
3	1	7	6	9	2	4	5	8
9	6	4	5	8	7	2	3	1
2	8	5	3	4	1	9	6	7

Hard Puzzle 227

9	3	8	7	6	5	2	4	1
6	7	5	4	1	2	9	3	8
2	4	1	9	8	3	7	6	5
3	1	2	6	7	8	5	9	4
7	6	4	3	5	9	1	8	2
5	8	9	2	4	1	3	7	6
4	9	3	1	2	6	8	5	7
1	5	6	8	9	7	4	2	3
8	2	7	5	3	4	6	1	9

Hard Puzzle 228

1	3	2	9	8	4	7	6	5
4	8	7	5	2	6	1	3	9
5	6	9	7	3	1	8	4	2
8	7	5	4	9	3	2	1	6
3	9	4	1	6	2	5	7	8
6	2	1	8	5	7	3	9	4
9	4	8	3	7	5	6	2	1
2	5	3	6	1	9	4	8	7
7	1	6	2	4	8	9	5	3

Hard Puzzle 229

3	6	9	1	8	2	7	4	5
8	1	7	6	5	4	9	3	2
4	5	2	9	3	7	1	6	8
9	8	1	3	7	6	5	2	4
7	3	6	2	4	5	8	9	1
5	2	4	8	1	9	6	7	3
1	4	3	7	6	8	2	5	9
2	7	5	4	9	1	3	8	6
6	9	8	5	2	3	4	1	7

Hard Puzzle 230

1	4	6	2	7	3	5	8	9
7	2	5	4	8	9	6	1	3
3	8	9	5	6	1	7	4	2
9	5	4	7	3	8	1	2	6
2	6	7	9	1	5	4	3	8
8	3	1	6	4	2	9	5	7
5	1	3	8	9	7	2	6	4
6	7	2	3	5	4	8	9	1
4	9	8	1	2	6	3	7	5

Hard Puzzle 231

9	7	2	5	3	4	1	8	6
1	4	3	8	2	6	5	7	9
8	6	5	1	7	9	4	3	2
7	9	4	3	1	5	6	2	8
5	8	6	2	9	7	3	1	4
2	3	1	6	4	8	9	5	7
4	1	8	9	5	2	7	6	3
3	2	9	7	6	1	8	4	5
6	5	7	4	8	3	2	9	1

Hard Puzzle 232

6	3	8	5	2	7	1	4	9
9	1	5	6	8	4	7	3	2
2	7	4	9	1	3	6	8	5
5	6	7	2	3	8	9	1	4
8	9	1	4	5	6	3	2	7
3	4	2	1	7	9	5	6	8
7	8	9	3	6	2	4	5	1
1	2	3	7	4	5	8	9	6
4	5	6	8	9	1	2	7	3

Hard Puzzle 233

7	8	1	5	4	9	6	2	3
3	6	5	8	1	2	4	7	9
9	2	4	7	6	3	5	1	8
2	7	9	4	5	8	1	3	6
4	1	8	6	3	7	2	9	5
5	3	6	9	2	1	7	8	4
6	9	2	1	8	4	3	5	7
8	4	3	2	7	5	9	6	1
1	5	7	3	9	6	8	4	2

Hard Puzzle 234

3	5	1	8	7	9	6	2	4
8	4	2	6	3	1	5	9	7
7	6	9	5	4	2	3	1	8
2	9	8	4	5	6	7	3	1
4	3	6	1	2	7	8	5	9
1	7	5	9	8	3	4	6	2
9	2	3	7	6	8	1	4	5
5	1	7	3	9	4	2	8	6
6	8	4	2	1	5	9	7	3

Hard Puzzle 235

2	6	9	1	5	4	7	3	8
4	8	1	3	2	7	5	6	9
5	3	7	9	6	8	2	4	1
3	7	6	5	4	1	9	8	2
8	5	2	6	3	9	1	7	4
1	9	4	7	8	2	3	5	6
7	1	5	8	9	6	4	2	3
6	4	3	2	1	5	8	9	7
9	2	8	4	7	3	6	1	5

Hard Puzzle 236

7	6	5	4	1	2	9	8	3
2	3	1	5	9	8	6	4	7
4	9	8	6	3	7	1	2	5
9	2	4	8	5	6	3	7	1
8	1	6	7	4	3	2	5	9
3	5	7	1	2	9	8	6	4
6	4	2	9	7	1	5	3	8
5	8	9	3	6	4	7	1	2
1	7	3	2	8	5	4	9	6

Hard Puzzle 237

3	5	7	2	1	6	9	8	4
1	9	8	5	4	3	2	7	6
4	2	6	8	9	7	5	3	1
5	4	2	6	8	9	3	1	7
6	1	3	7	2	5	8	4	9
7	8	9	4	3	1	6	5	2
2	6	1	3	7	8	4	9	5
9	3	5	1	6	4	7	2	8
8	7	4	9	5	2	1	6	3

Hard Puzzle 238

5	7	2	1	6	4	8	9	3
4	9	3	5	8	7	2	1	6
1	8	6	3	2	9	5	7	4
6	4	1	2	5	3	9	8	7
8	3	9	7	1	6	4	2	5
7	2	5	4	9	8	6	3	1
2	5	7	8	4	1	3	6	9
3	6	8	9	7	5	1	4	2
9	1	4	6	3	2	7	5	8

Hard Puzzle 239

1	8	9	4	5	6	2	7	3
6	2	5	7	3	8	9	1	4
7	4	3	1	9	2	8	5	6
2	3	4	6	8	7	5	9	1
8	9	7	3	1	5	6	4	2
5	6	1	2	4	9	3	8	7
4	5	2	8	6	1	7	3	9
9	1	6	5	7	3	4	2	8
3	7	8	9	2	4	1	6	5

Hard Puzzle 240

8	4	3	9	7	5	2	6	1
5	2	1	8	3	6	4	7	9
6	7	9	2	4	1	8	3	5
9	1	4	3	2	7	5	8	6
2	3	8	5	6	9	7	1	4
7	6	5	1	8	4	9	2	3
3	5	7	4	1	2	6	9	8
4	8	2	6	9	3	1	5	7
1	9	6	7	5	8	3	4	2

Hard Puzzle 241

7	1	8	6	9	2	5	3	4
9	3	2	5	4	8	7	6	1
5	4	6	1	7	3	9	8	2
6	8	1	9	3	5	4	2	7
2	7	9	8	1	4	3	5	6
4	5	3	2	6	7	8	1	9
3	6	5	7	2	9	1	4	8
8	2	7	4	5	1	6	9	3
1	9	4	3	8	6	2	7	5

Hard Puzzle 242

9	4	8	6	1	2	5	7	3
1	2	5	4	3	7	9	6	8
3	6	7	8	9	5	1	2	4
8	9	3	5	7	6	2	4	1
6	5	4	1	2	8	7	3	9
7	1	2	3	4	9	6	8	5
4	8	9	7	6	1	3	5	2
2	3	6	9	5	4	8	1	7
5	7	1	2	8	3	4	9	6

Hard Puzzle 243

2	4	5	3	8	6	1	9	7
7	1	9	2	4	5	6	8	3
8	3	6	7	1	9	4	2	5
5	9	4	1	6	3	2	7	8
3	2	1	8	5	7	9	4	6
6	7	8	9	2	4	5	3	1
1	5	3	4	9	8	7	6	2
9	6	7	5	3	2	8	1	4
4	8	2	6	7	1	3	5	9

Hard Puzzle 244

2	5	1	3	7	6	4	9	8
6	9	4	5	8	2	1	3	7
8	7	3	4	1	9	5	2	6
1	6	9	8	2	4	3	7	5
7	8	2	9	5	3	6	4	1
3	4	5	7	6	1	2	8	9
5	3	6	2	9	8	7	1	4
9	2	7	1	4	5	8	6	3
4	1	8	6	3	7	9	5	2

Hard Puzzle 245

8	7	6	1	3	9	4	2	5
4	2	9	8	6	5	7	3	1
5	3	1	2	7	4	6	9	8
9	1	5	4	2	7	8	6	3
3	6	8	5	9	1	2	4	7
7	4	2	3	8	6	1	5	9
6	8	7	9	4	3	5	1	2
2	5	3	6	1	8	9	7	4
1	9	4	7	5	2	3	8	6

Hard Puzzle 246

3	9	7	4	8	6	2	1	5
6	1	4	9	5	2	3	7	8
2	5	8	3	7	1	4	6	9
8	7	3	1	6	5	9	2	4
5	4	9	2	3	7	1	8	6
1	6	2	8	4	9	7	5	3
9	3	5	7	2	8	6	4	1
7	8	1	6	9	4	5	3	2
4	2	6	5	1	3	8	9	7

Hard Puzzle 247

4	7	1	2	6	9	3	8	5
2	6	9	5	3	8	7	4	1
5	8	3	4	7	1	9	6	2
9	4	5	3	1	2	8	7	6
6	3	8	9	5	7	2	1	4
7	1	2	6	8	4	5	3	9
8	9	4	7	2	6	1	5	3
1	5	6	8	9	3	4	2	7
3	2	7	1	4	5	6	9	8

Hard Puzzle 248

5	7	2	8	1	4	3	9	6
3	1	4	9	7	6	2	5	8
8	6	9	5	2	3	1	7	4
2	9	1	6	3	5	4	8	7
7	5	3	4	8	1	6	2	9
6	4	8	7	9	2	5	1	3
9	3	6	1	5	8	7	4	2
4	8	5	2	6	7	9	3	1
1	2	7	3	4	9	8	6	5

Hard Puzzle 249

1	3	7	8	6	2	5	4	9
2	4	8	5	9	1	7	6	3
9	5	6	7	3	4	1	2	8
6	9	5	2	4	7	8	3	1
7	8	2	3	1	9	6	5	4
4	1	3	6	5	8	2	9	7
8	7	4	9	2	5	3	1	6
5	6	1	4	7	3	9	8	2
3	2	9	1	8	6	4	7	5

Hard Puzzle 250

1	6	2	4	8	3	9	7	5
7	4	8	1	5	9	6	2	3
9	3	5	7	2	6	4	8	1
3	9	7	5	4	1	8	6	2
2	5	6	3	7	8	1	9	4
8	1	4	6	9	2	3	5	7
4	8	9	2	3	7	5	1	6
5	2	1	9	6	4	7	3	8
6	7	3	8	1	5	2	4	9

Made in the USA
Las Vegas, NV
09 November 2024

11446661R00109